Evolution of Library Liaisons

SPEC Kits

Supporting Effective Library Management for Over 40 Years

Committed to assisting research and academic libraries in the continuous improvement of management systems, ARL has worked since 1970 to gather and disseminate the best practices for library needs. As part of its commitment, ARL maintains an active publications program best known for its SPEC Kits. Through the Collaborative Research/Writing Program, librarians work with ARL staff to design SPEC surveys and write publications. Originally established as an information source for ARL member libraries, the SPEC Kit series has grown to serve the needs of the library community worldwide.

What are SPEC Kits?

SPEC Kits contain the most valuable, up-to-date information on the latest issues of concern to libraries and librarians today. They are the result of a systematic survey of ARL member libraries on a particular topic related to current practice in the field. Each SPEC Kit contains an executive summary of the survey results; survey questions with tallies and selected comments; the best representative documents from survey participants, such as policies, procedures, handbooks, guidelines, Web sites, records, brochures, and statements; and a selected reading list—both print and online sources—containing the most current literature available on the topic for further study.

Subscribe to SPEC Kits

Subscribers tell us that the information contained in SPEC Kits is valuable to a variety of users, both inside and outside the library. SPEC Kit purchasers use the documentation found in SPEC Kits as a point of departure for research and problem solving because they lend immediate authority to proposals and set standards for designing programs or writing procedure statements. SPEC Kits also function as an important reference tool for library administrators, staff, students, and professionals in allied disciplines who may not have access to this kind of information.

SPEC Kits are available in print and online. The executive summary for each kit after December 1993 can be accessed online free of charge. For more information visit: **http://www.arl.org/publications-resources**.

SPEC Kit 349

Evolution of Library Liaisons
November 2015

Rebecca K. Miller

Pennsylvania State University

Lauren Pressley

University of Washington

ASSOCIATION OF RESEARCH LIBRARIES®

SURVEY RESULTS

EXECUTIVE SUMMARY

Introduction

As research libraries develop new directions and priorities in response to changing needs of the students, faculty, researchers, and staff at their institutions, the role of library liaisons continues to shift and evolve. Library liaisons traditionally have helped support academic departments, faculty, and students through outreach and communication, teaching one-shot instruction sessions, offering customized research consultations, and participating in disciplinary collection development. However, in her 2014 report *Leveraging the Liaison Model*, Anne Kenney writes that many research libraries are beginning "to shift the focus away from the work of librarians to that of scholars and to develop engagement strategies based on their needs and success indicators."[1] Overall, Kenney notes that the current liaison model simply does not meet the needs of the twenty-first century university and research library. While many libraries are developing new strategies for evolving their liaison programs in order to meet new challenges in research, scholarship, and engagement, there are unanswered questions about how successful, impactful, and effective liaison programs can be developed and supported.

The purpose of this survey was to gather data about the evolving role of the library liaison and the shifting goals and strategies of liaison programs at ARL member libraries. In particular, to identify emerging trends and themes in the changes occurring in the library liaison model and the factors that influence these changes on an institutional level. Because each institution and its needs are unique, this survey focused on not only the specific changes occurring in liaison programs, but also the general conditions that contribute to both the need and support for these changes.

This survey was distributed to the 124 ARL member libraries in July 2015. Seventy members (57%) provided seventy-two responses by the August 12, 2015 deadline, and the responses summarized here continue to indicate that the evolving liaison model is a critical component in ARL member libraries' ability to meet the broad challenges of today's research libraries and take advantage of opportunities to move in new strategic directions. By providing data points, examples, and trends that will contribute to the growth and direction of liaison services, we hope that this report will contribute to library leaders' ability to support their surrounding community in new and exciting ways.

Evolution of Liaison Roles

Background research reveals that there is no shortage of literature related to the topic of liaison services in all types of libraries. Indeed, as the third SPEC Kit devoted to liaison services, this publication has the opportunity to compare data and trends from the 1992 and 2007 SPEC surveys with the data gathered in 2015. The 1992 report, SPEC Kit 189, focused on defining practices, definitions, and policies of library liaisons, but in her summary, author Gail Latta noted that "effort should be made to continue exploring non-traditional and expanded roles for liaisons, as contributing members of research teams and instructional programs."[2] Latta presciently identified one of the major shifts in liaison services when writing that, "as the physical collection becomes less central, the user is becoming the focus of library services."[3] These observations also resonated with the authors of the 2007 report, SPEC Kit 301, as they noted a general increase in attention given to services beyond collection development, including information literacy instruction, scholarly communication education, and digital project consulting.[4]

Both the 1992 and 2007 reports provide evidence that liaison services represent one of the most dynamic areas of library organizations, constantly evolving in response to or in anticipation of the surrounding communities' activities, needs, and expectations. This survey explores the directions of these shifts. However, it also considers what these shifts mean for the professionals filling the role of library liaison and the leaders who are helping to define, guide, and assess the success of library liaison programs.

Background of Liaison Services

Sixty-seven respondents (93%) indicated that their library's organizational structure includes librarians or other library staff with liaison responsibilities. Of the five respondents that indicated they did not have library liaisons, three are non-academic libraries, in which liaison services are not relevant. Several respondents indicated that, while their organization includes library liaisons, they may call these positions something different or use a team-based approach to work with their surrounding communities. Many respondents placed the birth of their liaison programs prior to or during the 1960s and 1970s, but acknowledge that the general beginnings of the programs are unclear and that their labels and scopes have changed over time. A general trend seems to point to an evolution from subject specialists, bibliographers, and selectors in the early days of liaison activities to what a number of libraries are now framing as "engagement" facilitators.

Because of the overall uncertainty about the start of many libraries' liaison services and programs, responses to questions about how these liaison roles originally were determined indicate that there are a lot of unknowns about the process. Fifty-six respondents (84%) identified a library administrative decision as the manner in which the roles were determined, and 48 (73%) identified libraries' perceived needs of departments as a factor in the role-defining and decision-making process.

Liaison Roles

As the liaison role has shifted over time, so have the staffing categories, qualifications, and requirements of the individuals who fill these roles. Of the 67 libraries that have staff in liaison roles, only 13 (19%) responded that every professional librarian in their institution held liaison responsibilities. The majority of respondents (54 or 81%) indicated that some professional librarians' job descriptions included liaison duties and some did not. At organizations where this mix of responsibilities occurs, librarians typically assume liaison duties for a number of reasons, including being hired into a liaison-specific role, having prior experiences, education, or interest in a subject area or liaison role, and serving in a public services position where outreach is considered a primary component of the position. Many library staff members who are not professional librarians are also assuming liaison duties. Forty-two of the responding libraries (63%) indicated that some other professionals, support staff, and other library staff are serving in the role of liaison. Examples of other types of positions taking on liaison duties include archivist, bioinformationist, curator, director of communications and outreach, GIS analyst, diversity intern, library assistant/specialist/technician, research assistants, and language experts.

While a variety of staffing categories may be given liaison responsibilities, the responding libraries converge on several key qualifications for library liaisons. Although 42 libraries employ non-librarians in liaison roles, sixty-four respondents (99%) indicated that an MLS from an accredited school is a moderate to very important qualification; 44 of those (68%) reported the MLS is a "very important" qualification. In comparison, only four respondents (6%) listed a second master's degree as a "very important" qualification. Sixty-three (96%) identified "demonstrated communication skills" as a moderate to very important qualification for liaisons, with 40 (61%) listing these skills in the "very important" category. Interestingly, respondents to the 1992 survey also identified communication skills as a key qualification for library liaisons, and one that should be addressed in graduate degree programs in library science. Other qualifications that were identified multiple times in the current survey include collaborative/teamwork skills, user-centered focus, and teaching skills. Overwhelmingly, respondents regard subject expertise as the primary reason for deciding how a liaison receives a department assignment (65 responses or 97%). Forty-five (67%) make decisions based on the liaison's position, and many libraries consider additional criteria, including a specific need or gap in the library's coverage of departments, and the liaison's interest or passion.

Liaison Assignments

There appears to be a wide spectrum of how liaison responsibilities are carried out in ARL member institutions. While there are some positions completely devoted to liaison work, in their responses to questions about liaison duties and percentages of liaison duties most respondents indicated that liaison responsibilities are often added to existing positions in order to help fill a need, help a professional grow in his or her position, or to help a professional meet a particular interest.

The number of departments assigned to a liaison ranges from one to 100, but in only seventeen libraries (25%) do all liaisons work with more than one department. Explaining the assignment of liaison responsibilities can be complicated, since there is also a wide variety of organizational structures within respondents' parent institutions. One respondent commented that questions about departmental assignments are difficult to answer because it "depends on how you define departments...some liaisons are assigned to schools within universities that may consist of multiple departments." Even so, there is evidence of a real effort among ARL libraries to ensure that various groups that comprise the surrounding community be paired with a liaison; 59 respondents (88%) have assigned a library liaison to every department within their institution or community. Within the departments, 100% of the responding libraries provide services for or reach out directly to teaching and research faculty. The majority of libraries also provide services for other faculty (99%), graduate teaching assistants and graduate students (96%), undergraduate students (94%), administrative staff (88%), and other community members, including alumni, community members (public), fellows, visiting researchers, and administrators. These numbers show

a significant increase since 2007 in the support offered for undergraduates and administrative staff, when around three quarters of the responding libraries offered services for these groups.

Many libraries are also evolving toward creating liaison relationships beyond academic departments. The 1992 and 2007 surveys focused primarily on academic departments, but over half of the respondents to the current survey indicated that their libraries have developed liaison relationships with non-academic departments such as academic computing offices, athletics, career centers, centers for teaching and learning, educational technology groups, student affairs, and diversity groups. Further, when asked if library liaisons work as partners, rather than full-fledged liaisons, with various non-academic departments, 54 respondents (89%) identified centers for teaching and learning as a partner with which library liaisons work. The majority of respondents also identified information technology (74%), student affairs (67%), offices for institutional research (64%), offices of accessibility (57%), and offices of sponsored programs (56%) as partners with which library liaisons often work.

Perhaps because of this evolution in the types and numbers of departments that are assigned to library liaisons or with which library liaisons work as collaborative partners, data from the 1992, 2007, and 2015 surveys show that liaisons are clearly working with an increasing number of stakeholders. In 1992, the largest number of departments assigned to one liaison was 12, and in 2007, the largest number was 31. In 2015, the largest number is 100. While this number is definitely an outlier, since only one response included a number this high for number of departments assigned to one liaison, 23% of the respondents indicated that 10 or more departments have been assigned to a single liaison.

Department Participation and Communication

While this survey established that ARL libraries are creating support for an increasing number of departments within their communities, there is still some question over how often liaison services are used. Nearly half of the have assigned indicated that departments within their communities do not take advantage of liaison services. Several remarked that, while most of the departments that are offered liaison services use them in some way, the extent of participation varies among departments. Nearly all survey respondents (96%) are actively seeking ways to increase participation from departments, and the rest are planning to soon. Again, nearly all of the responding libraries encourage liaisons to attend departmental meetings (98%) and actively market liaison services (97%). Other methods that ARL libraries are using to actively increase participation from departments include attending orientations and other campus events, co-authoring papers and presentations, collaborative teaching opportunities, social media, inviting departments to library events, and embedding librarians in various department-related opportunities.

A recognized method of increasing departmental participation is ensuring that libraries fully understand the needs of the communities that they serve. All of the responding libraries use communication, such as conversation, email, or other methods, with faculty, students, and researchers to attempt to assess needs and understand departmental priorities. Forty-nine libraries (75%) also use documentation from departments, such as strategic plans and promotion and tenure guidelines for this purpose, and 47 (72%) have surveyed faculty, students, and researchers to gain insight into their work. Examples of other methods that library liaisons are using to better understand departmental needs include: bibliometric analysis of faculty publications, university-level strategic plans, curriculum review, town halls, focus groups, LibQUAL+®, and collaborative research. Survey responses indicate that many libraries are using a diverse portfolio of methods to investigate community needs, which enables them to be both reactive and proactive when identifying new areas of support for library liaisons.

Liaison Core Duties and Services
The definition and core duties of a library liaison have changed fairly dramatically over the past two decades. The 2007 SPEC Kit on liaison services reviewed the 1992 and 2001 RUSA guidelines for liaisons, noting that in 1992, the RUSA guidelines mainly focused on the liaison's responsibility to gather information for collection development.[5] The 2001 RUSA guidelines

expanded to include five components: three still centering around collection development and two dealing with public relations and communication with the surrounding community. RUSA's guidelines were updated again in 2010 and include a wide variety of activities related to liaison work in academic libraries, including developing collections, identifying users, and activities such as participating in campus organizations and encouraging wide library use.[6]

In this survey, nearly all the responding libraries identified the following as core liaison duties: providing one-on-one research consultations (99%), managing library collections in disciplinary areas (97%), outreach and communication (97%), and teaching one-shot information literacy sessions (96%). The majority of respondents indicated an additional suite of liaison core duties, including providing consulting on scholarly communication issues (82%), reporting news from disciplinary departments back to the library (79%), embedding in discipline-based courses (76%), providing data management support and consulting (63%), and regularly staffing the reference desk (61%). Nearly half of the respondents (46%) listed additional core duties taken on by their liaisons. Listed multiple times were citation analysis and impact metrics, using and teaching new technology tools, digital scholarship support, and literature review help.

The full menu of services offered by liaisons at ARL libraries covers a wide breadth of support areas. In 2007, primary areas of liaison services included departmental outreach, communication of departmental needs back to the library, reference, collection development, library instruction, and scholarly communication education. Each of these areas remains at the top of the current menu of liaison services (90% of all respondents named all of these services). However, the majority of respondents also named at least eight additional services that are now on the liaison menu: assistance with scholarly impact and metrics (88%), promotion of institutional repository (83%), consultation on open access issues (82%), creating web-based learning objects (80%), e-research support (80%), data management support (79%), consultation on intellectual property issues (71%), and new literacies education (58%). Examples of other services are data visualization support, GIS support, help with systematic reviews, text mining, and promotion of open access journal development.

It is clear that each liaison doesn't offer every one of these areas of support, and that they often develop functional areas of support in addition to disciplinary areas of support. A number of respondents indicated that liaisons are not expected to meet all of the diverse needs of their departments. Rather, they are expected to leverage the strengths of other liaisons within their library, work collaboratively with other liaisons, and act as a connector between their departments and other library liaisons or community partners who may be able to help them move forward on projects and resolve complicated teaching and research situations. We continue to see this more collaborative method of work emerge through responses to questions about how library liaisons define their roles, communicate with each other, grow in their professional roles, and assess and evaluate their work and the success of entire liaison programs.

Policies and Guidelines

This expansion of liaison roles and services can make it difficult to define what, precisely, it means to be a library liaison. Even when core duties are articulated and programs are structured, many libraries find it helpful to develop policies and guidelines that advise liaison work. Nearly three-quarters of the responding libraries (47) have written policies or definitions that describe liaison work. Fewer libraries (36 or 56%) have written policies governing the functions, activities, and responsibilities of library liaisons. Liaisons continue to take a major role in defining their own work, as seen in the 55 libraries (83%) where liaisons participate in establishing the policies that do govern their activities. In 42 libraries (65%), liaisons have written goals and objectives that guide their activities, as well. Overall, this data demonstrates that liaisons generally have agency and some level of independence in defining their own roles, areas of expertise, and goals.

Administration, Communication, and Workflow

As the need to work together and leverage different individuals' expertise continues to emerge within library liaison programs, it becomes more important for liaisons and those who lead liaison programs to develop methods and strategies for communication and collaboration. Indeed nearly all of the survey respondents (97%) indicated that they actively encourage liaisons to share expertise and solve problems collaboratively. The few libraries that do not yet encourage team-based work are planning to start doing so soon. A number of respondents mentioned that collaborative work goes beyond liaison collaboration, and actually ends up looking more like a three-way conversation, including the faculty/researcher role, the library liaison, and a functional specialist who may focus on an area such as data, copyright, or GIS. Additionally, some library organizational structures bring subject and functional specialists into one, shared department where these sorts of conversations and collaborations are able to take place, and at least one respondent discussed using project-based teams that encourage various library liaisons and specialists to work together to support specific projects or initiatives.

The coordination and facilitation of library liaisons within the overall library structure has a significant impact on the ability of liaisons to form the sorts of teams and collaborations that enable them to meet the emerging needs of the surrounding communities. Survey responses indicate there is no consistent method of administering and facilitating liaison programs, though. Within the wide spectrum of methods used to organize and administer liaison programs, the most frequently used is self-administration by each liaison (27 responses or 41%). Fewer libraries use any sort of central administration structure. Nine libraries (14%) use a central liaison coordinator or manager, six (9%) use a liaison committee, and four (6%) manage liaisons through central administration. Nearly one third of the responding libraries use a unique organizational and administrative structure, examples of which often include liaisons reporting within multiple departments and to multiple supervisors, a combination of self-directed and central management, and various types of liaison leadership teams. Just as liaison duties have expanded and become more complex, the reporting lines and administrative structures of liaison roles and programs have also become more complex and messier. For comparison, in the 2007 report, about half of the responding libraries reported their liaison programs as self-directed and a quarter reported their liaison programs as centrally administered.

In light of the data regarding the management of liaison programs, it is not surprising that the current survey indicates that liaisons report to supervisors in nearly every possible area of library work. At 40 of the responding libraries (60%) liaisons simply report to their respective department heads. At 29 libraries (43%) there are different reporting lines for different liaisons, which supports the idea that the central management or coordination of liaison programs is increasingly challenging. Part of this challenge, then, also includes communication between library decision makers and liaisons. Fifty-three respondents offered various examples of how this communication occurs within their libraries, including regular group meetings between administrators and liaisons, one-on-one meetings between administrators and liaisons, email, the use of an intranet, library administrator and liaison co-participation on library committees, liaison participation in strategic planning initiatives, regular collection of data and statistics, and other informal methods of communication. It is significant to note that multiple libraries reported that there is no effective method of this sort of communication in place or that it is currently being reviewed or explored within those libraries.

Even though communication between library liaisons and library decision makers can look messy, many libraries have developed effective methods for liaisons to communicate with each other about projects, issues, and best practices. Most respondents mentioned regular departmental meetings as an effective method for sharing ideas and knowledge. Others discussed more focused learning opportunities, such as teaching communities, brown bags, symposia and fora, retreats, internal workshops, journal clubs, and disciplinary or subject-based teams.

Training and Professional Development

Structured training and professional development also becomes an important discussion as liaison roles expand and shift. Nearly all the responding libraries (91%) provide training for new library liaisons. This data is consistent with findings from the 2007 survey on liaison services, which also found that nearly all

libraries provide some sort of training for new liaisons, although about one fifth of these training opportunities were unstructured or informal. In the current survey, several respondents still mentioned that training opportunities are unstructured or informal, but many others indicated that their liaison training is "robust" or "rigorous." For many libraries, the training program appears to be customized to the liaison and the tools, skill set, and knowledge that each one will need to work with his or her assigned groups. Respondents often mentioned mentoring as a large part of the training process, and many also mentioned specific tools that new liaisons needed training on, including the Open Access Harvester tool, LibGuides, LibAnalytics, data management tools, institutional repositories, ORCID, and local online ordering systems. General areas of training mentioned multiple times include data management, scholarly communication, collections, reference, instruction and information literacy, special disciplinary topics, and outreach. Of the 51 responses received regarding new liaison training, only two specifically identified areas of "soft" skills, such as presentation skills or communication skills. This is a particularly interesting finding, since communication skills ranks so highly as a key qualification for library liaisons.

For ongoing professional development opportunities, nearly all the responding libraries (62 or 97%) offer library liaisons dedicated funding and support for attending conferences. The majority of libraries also offer continuing education and professional development in the form of internal cross-training (94%), funding for external workshops (92%), and participation in formal degree and certificate programs (70%). Other types of continuing education and development in which library liaisons participate include dedicated research days, web-based tools like lynda.com, and internally developed training programs.

Evaluation of Liaisons and Programs

Measuring the success of individual liaisons and entire liaison programs represents one area that has been identified as very challenging within relevant library literature. Overall, the majority of survey respondents indicated that the responsibility of evaluating individual liaisons on their liaison responsibilities falls to a variety of supervisors. In nearly half of the responding libraries, the liaison's primary supervisor provides the main evaluation. However, nineteen libraries (28%) indicated that, while a liaison's primary supervisor conducts the evaluation, other library leaders provide input to the evaluation. Half of the respondents reported that the liaison's evaluation is completed based on evaluation criteria that include the liaison functions. Nearly a third reported that liaisons and their supervisors set goals on which the liaisons are evaluated. Other libraries use peer review and quantitative data to inform the evaluation of individual liaisons' success.

Sixty-three of the responding libraries (94%) do collect statistics that document liaison activities, which can be used to gain insight on the effectiveness of both individual liaisons and entire liaison programs. Most libraries collect data beyond the required ARL statistics in order to gain a broader view of the activities conducted through liaison relationships. The types of liaison activities on which statistics are collected at most responding libraries include classes and instruction sessions, research consultations, reference questions, outreach activities, number of searches conducted, collection development spending, circulation data, grant funding received, number of web-based learning objects created, and uses of objects created.

Beyond collection of these types of statistics, fewer libraries consistently evaluate the effectiveness of the overall liaison program. In fact, responses were evenly split between those libraries that do conduct formal evaluations of liaison programs (32 or 49%) and those that do not (34 or 51%). These numbers are consistent with the findings from the 2007 report; however, current data suggests that many libraries are moving beyond collecting numbers, which was the main means of evaluation reported in the 2007 SPEC Kit, and are starting to try to measure the overall impact of their liaison programs. Over half of the current survey's responding libraries (63%) conduct user surveys about their liaison programs, and over a third (38%) interview members of their constituent departments. About a quarter (28%) also document departmental meetings attended by librarians, conduct focus groups, and use other methods of exploring the impact of their programs, including external reviews

with community leaders, working with library science graduate students to review liaison programs, and using matrices to gauge overall engagement.

As libraries think about how to evaluate the impact of their programs, they look for a number of different things as indicators of success. Nearly all the responding libraries use the development of new partnerships across campus as a major indicator of success (58 or 95%). The majority of libraries also look at the growth rate of research consultations (85%) and classes (80%) as indicators of success. A third also use professional recognition (39%), the retention of liaisons (33%), and additional funding from the university or institution (31%) as further indicators of liaison program success.

Challenges and Benefits

In the 2007 survey on liaison services, the top three challenges for liaisons were described as establishing and maintaining contact with faculty, time constraints and competing responsibilities for liaisons, and internal and external communication. The current survey data indicate that these are still challenges, and perhaps even more so. The two words that appeared most frequently in responses about the top challenges for library liaisons were "balance" and "scalability." Library liaisons are balancing a workload that often includes responsibilities beyond liaison activities, and are also trying to balance the more traditional types of liaison work, such as reference consultations and collection management, with growing new areas of liaison engagement, such as scholarly communication and data management consulting. A number of respondents mentioned that getting liaisons to understand these new areas of service and integrate them into the liaison role is a challenge, as it requires constant learning, growing, and training. Perhaps because of this, many respondents also mentioned communication issues, inconsistency within liaison programs, and a lack of understanding about the value and abilities of liaisons both internally and externally as major challenges. One respondent succinctly stated that the challenges with governing and growing liaison programs can fit into three categories: people, time, and money.

Although there are clear challenges as liaison programs move into new and uncharted territory, the benefits of these programs remain clear. Library liaisons provide a "human face" for the library and ultimately allow libraries to engage more deeply in the life of the surrounding community and better understand that community's needs and trajectories. Many respondents reported that library liaisons "keep the library relevant" because they are engaged in relationships and partnerships that enable the library to grow and evolve in appropriate and valuable directions.

Discussion

After comparing data from the 1992, 2007, and current surveys on library liaisons, it is clear that liaison services and programs represent some of the most visibly evolving components of twenty-first century libraries. Some of the major areas of change for library liaisons include skill sets, core duties and responsibilities, stakeholders, methods of internal and external communication and collaboration, and the definition of impact and success. Much has changed over the previous twenty-three years, and we can anticipate that this rate of change will continue as libraries work with new partners and embrace new roles within their communities. When asked if the liaison role at their institution has undergone major changes recently, three-quarters of the respondents answered in the affirmative. Twelve others (18%) responded that changes were currently in process or about to happen. In addition to changes to core duties and responsibilities, respondents identified a number of significant changes to services. Many mentioned that liaisons were decreasing or completely jettisoning reference desk hours, embracing new modes of research, scholarship, and literacies, exploring and gaining expertise in sophisticated technology, and working collaboratively to leverage the expertise of internal and external partners.

These changes have been driven by a number of factors that are fairly consistent among responding libraries. Fifty respondents (82%) reported that changes to the liaison role have been driven by the changing landscape of scholarship and publication. Forty-two libraries (69%) developed changes based on the identification of new needs within the community, and roughly half of the responding libraries initiated liaison changes because of new library leadership. Other catalysts of change include changes in

various disciplines, library reorganizations, reduced staffing, and changes in federal policies. Liaisons and administrators appear to be working together to initiate changes to liaison roles, an aspect of this evolution that situates liaisons at the center of rapid and profound change in research and higher education. The data from this survey plainly demonstrate library liaisons' facility for growing in new directions in order to enhance the libraries' value and reach. However, it is less clear that liaisons are working to shift some responsibilities in order to embrace new ones. About half of the respondents reported that liaisons have relinquished responsibilities to take on new ones. A quarter reported that no liaison duties have been relinquished, but that there is a plan to shift responsibilities over the next 1 to 3 years. Ten libraries (16%) reported no plans to formally shift liaison responsibilities in order to make room for new areas of growth. The two most commonly reported responsibilities that have been shifted away from library liaisons include staffing public service points and in-depth collection development. This becomes possible as libraries use demand driven acquisition and centralize collections work and create alternate staffing models for public service points. Library liaisons are reaching new stakeholders, participating in new conversations, and developing new areas of expertise. It will be critical for library administrators and liaisons to continue to consider ways that liaisons can shift responsibilities in order to evolve and innovate.

Conclusion

One respondent commented that "liaisons are more important than ever in the work we are doing to support campus priorities and strategic directions." Another observed that liaison roles, even within a single library, are "nuanced...given the degree of variability across units, and across individual approaches to liaison roles." The data from this survey show that successful liaisons are both independent and collaborative workers, proactive rather than reactive, and discriminating in the scope of their work, yet also flexible and open to new areas of working and partnering. As libraries move to outcomes-based assessment and strive to measure the impact of their work, it becomes increasingly important for liaisons to participate in these conversations and articulate their goals and ideas for measuring progress or success. In 1992, SPEC Kit 189 called for library liaisons to "explore non-traditional and expanded roles" and to act as "contributing members of research teams and instructional programs."[7] It feels safe to write that this is exactly the direction in which the library liaison role has evolved, and that liaisons are now partnering in ways that were unimaginable twenty-three years ago. At this point in time, library liaisons have the opportunity and resources to move beyond a "contributing" role in these partnerships. Data from the current survey provide strong evidence that liaisons are proactively leading community conversations and initiatives in the areas of data management, teaching and learning, and scholarly communication. We will continue to see the liaison role shift and evolve, as library liaisons move from contributing partners to full-fledged leaders in the education and research enterprise.

Endnotes

1. Kenney, Anne R. *Leveraging the Liaison Model: From Defining 21st Century Research Libraries to Implementing 21st Century Research Universities.* Ithaka S+R, New York: Ithaka S+R, March 2014.

2. Latta, Gail F. *Liaison Services in ARL Libraries.* SPEC Kit 189. Washington, DC: Association of Research Libraries, November/December 1992.

3. Ibid.

4. Logue, Susan, John Ballestro, Andrea Imre, and Julie Arendt. *Liaison Services.* SPEC Kit 301, Washington, DC: Association of Research Libraries, October 2007.

5. Ibid.

6. Reference and User Services Association. "Guidelines for Liaison Work in Managing Collections and Services." Accessed October 29, 2015. http://www.ala.org/rusa/resources/guidelines/guidelinesliaison

7. Latta, *Liaison Services in ARL Libraries.*

SURVEY QUESTIONS AND RESPONSES

The SPEC Survey on the Evolution of Library Liaisons was designed by **Rebecca K. Miller,** Head of Library Learning Services at Pennsylvania State University Libraries, and **Lauren Pressley,** Director of the University of Washington Tacoma Library and Associate Dean of University Libraries at the University of Washington. These results are based on 72 responses from 70 of the 124 ARL member libraries (57%) by the deadline of August 12, 2015. The survey's introductory text and questions are reproduced below, followed by the response data and selected comments from the respondents.

As research libraries develop new directions and priorities in response to changing needs of the students, faculty, researchers, and staff at their institutions, the role of library liaisons continues to shift and evolve. Library liaisons traditionally have helped support academic departments, faculty, and students through outreach and communication, teaching one-shot instruction sessions, offering customized research consultations, and participating in disciplinary collection development. However, in her 2014 report *Leveraging the Liaison Model,* Anne Kenney writes that many research libraries are beginning "to shift the focus away from the work of librarians to that of scholars and to develop engagement strategies based on their needs and success indicators" (p. 4). Overall, Kenney notes that the current liaison model simply does not meet the needs of the twenty-first century university and research library. While many libraries are developing new strategies for evolving their liaison programs in order to meet new challenges in research, scholarship, and engagement, there are unanswered questions about how successful, impactful, and effective liaison programs can be developed and supported.

The purpose of this survey is to gather data about the evolving role of the library liaison and the shifting goals and strategies of liaison programs at ARL member libraries. In particular, this survey will identify emerging trends and themes in the changes occurring in the library liaison model and attempt to discover the factors that influence these changes on an institutional level. Because each institution and its needs are unique, this survey focuses on not only the specific changes occurring in liaison programs, but also the general conditions that contribute to both the need and support for these changes.

The evolving liaison model is a critical component in ARL member libraries' ability to meet the broad challenges of today's research libraries and take advantage of opportunities to move in new strategic directions. This survey will contribute to library leaders' ability to support their surrounding community in new ways by providing data points, examples, and trends that will contribute to the growth and direction of liaison services.

BACKGROUND

1. Does your library's organizational structure include librarians or other library staff whose job duties include liaison responsibilities as described in the introduction? N=72

    Yes   67   93%
    No   5   7%

    Comments N=4

    ### Answered Yes N=2

    > About two dozen librarians have subject librarian/liaison work as their primary assignment, and another dozen do some liaison work on a secondary basis (typically with contact at one campus department). This is out of about 80 librarians.

    > They are no longer called liaisons.

    ### Answered No N=2

    > Reference librarians teach classes and research orientations open to the general public in use of the library's collections. The library also has a division that offers job-related training, much of which is made available to the wider library community.

    > We moved away from the liaison model in 2009. Since that time, the library has been operating with a team-based model that depends on functional specialization (as opposed to disciplinary specialization, which is what we used to have in the liaison model).

    If yes, please complete the survey.

    If no, please answer one more question, then submit the survey.

NO LIBRARY LIAISONS

2. Is there anyone who serves as the library's primary contact with faculty, researchers, or students at your institution? N=5

    Yes   1   20%
    No   4   80%

    If yes, please briefly describe their position(s) and role(s). N=1

    > Manager Reference and Instruction Service

    ### Additional Comments N=4

    > All five of our strategic teams have interactions with faculty (some more than others).

As a national library, we don't directly serve faculty or students and most researchers who use our services have a primary library.

The library is not at a degree-granting institution.

This role is changed amongst various roles in the library.

PROGRAM BEGINNINGS

3. In what year did your library begin offering liaison services? N=66

Range: 1890 to 2012

Year	Responses
Pre-1960	13
1960s	5
1970s	10
1980s	10
1990s	14
2000s	12
2010s	2

Comments N=53

Pre-1960

Can't pinpoint the year since we have always had engagement models with faculty, students, and departments; the use of the term became more prominent in around 2008.

Evolved out of decades of previous systems of subject and bibliographic librarians.

Good question! Not sure!!

It seems that we have been providing these services for at least 40 years.

Liaison service has been in place for as long as anyone here can remember.

Library liaisons may have been present as far as back as the 18th century.

The first librarian hired by the Libraries was the Chemistry Librarian, in 1947, and that individual served as a direct liaison to the Department of Chemistry.

The library has always had liaison type role (1930).

This year (1890) relates to the first established subject library.

Very long ago.

We have always had librarians who fulfilled the traditional subject librarian/liaison role. In 2011 we made a deliberate decision to move toward an engaged librarian framework.

We've had liaisons as long as anyone here can remember. Formerly, we had separate subject libraries, although many were located in the main library building. These were merged into a general reference department several decades ago, with the subject librarians retaining their liaison roles in addition to providing general reference service and instruction.

1960s

Prior to 1971, which is the furthest back our institutional memory goes.

The library has always offered these services (1965).

This has evolved over decades, but some form of liaison activity has existed for at least 50 years.

We've always had liaison services (1965), but we have recently realigned the liaison program to give greater emphasis to the liaison work (2015).

We have had this model for many decades and the best guess is that some form of this approach existed as far back as the 1960s

1970s

Columbia Libraries commissioned Booz, Allen, Hamilton, Inc. to propose a new library staffing model in 1973. The result included recommendations about disciplinary divisions—humanities, science, and social science—including subject specialists. The plan was implemented around 1975.

It is very difficult to pinpoint the exact year we began offering liaison services (1970s?). I am certain that the library has had subject experts since the 1950s.

The date, 1979, corresponds to the establishment of university-wide library liaison assignments. Two branch libraries (Design and Textiles) were established in the 1940s, and one (Natural Resources) was established in 1970. These branch libraries were and continue to be staffed by librarians serving faculty and students in those disciplines. The Veterinary Medicine Library opened in 1981 with liaison services.

The inception of the model pre-dates the tenure of anyone working in the library. It goes well back into the last quarter of the 20th century.

This (1974) is an estimate as that was the first recorded liaison activities.

This (1975) is approximately the date. It occurred sometime in the mid 70s.

University Libraries started hiring more subject librarians in the late 1960s to take an active role in collection development. In mid-1970s more were hired to provide subject-based reference services.

We know it has been in place at least since the mid-1970s. As far as anyone knows, liaisons have always been part of the library's services.

1980s

Date (1985) is approximate.

I'm not sure of the actual year. I've heard sometime in the 80s.

Liaison services have been a longstanding part of the library's professional practice since at least the early 1980s.

Our Health Sciences Library has been officially offering liaison services since 1982. Prior to 1982, reference department librarians were assigned health affairs schools to focus on but they did not have the time to do outreach or provide special services to groups. This was during a time when there was a high level of reference desk activity and mediated searching. In 1982, a separate Information Management Education Services department was formed and instructional outreach began. University Library began in 2009–2010 academic year.

Prior to 1981, we had subject specialist librarians assigned to our branch libraries (predominantly in the sciences), with a team of "bibliographers" managing selection in other areas. In 1981, additional librarians were assigned roles for the humanities and social sciences.

The liaison program has undergone several transformations since 1984. There has not been one continuous organizational structure.

The year (1980) is an estimated figure. We have been offering liaison services for a long time.

Traditional liaison services to academic departments have been in place since at least 1980.

1990s

In 1992, public services librarians were given the option of remaining reference librarians (generalists) or becoming subject specialists where they were assigned subject area(s). Subject specialists provided subject-specific instruction and reference as well as performing collection development responsibilities for their assigned subject area(s).

Liaison Services came about as a consequence of combining separate subject collections, organized by floor, into one single library.

Much has changed. In 1999, this model was adopted in one or more branch libraries. Now our library has merged the branches into one library and reorganized into service-based programs, one of which is the Academic Liaison Program (ALP), established in 2012.

Specific date is not available, although 1999 saw a combining of liaison/outreach, collection development, and instruction activities.

The Health Science Center Library fully implemented its liaison librarian program in 1999, however the HSCL had librarians serving ex officio on the College of Medicine Curriculum committee (1992–) and Colleges of Dentistry and Nursing in 2006. These activities, along with strategic planning, served as impetus for the formal liaison librarian program.

The program began in the health sciences in 1991 or earlier and expanded to the rest of the colleges in 2013.

The year is approximate (1999). Before that, we had subject librarians, but it was around 1999/2000, that a librarian was put in charge of an official liaison program and all librarians were required to be liaisons.

There were liaison activities occurring before this time, but the approach was formalized in 1992.

We had several librarians doing liaison work from the mid-1980s on, but 1997 was the year all subject librarians started doing it.

We had subject librarians for many years, but started a formal "college librarian" program in 1994.

2000s

Estimated timeframe (2004)

However, we had subject librarians and even bibliographers going far back before 2004.

In 2004, the program began, but was in the developmental stages. Around 2007, the program became a more formalized, structured program.

The job title "liaison librarian" started being used in 2007. Prior to that, librarians were subject specialists.

The library had a traditional bibliographer/reference department model in place until 2007, when a new liaison program was created. Prior to 2007, bibliographers and special collections-related staff served as liaisons to academic departments. Instruction was the purview of the reference department.

There had previously been a number of people who served in a liaison capacity, but the more "formal" removal of bibliographers happened around this time (early 2000s).

This is a little fuzzy (2006). It has been a gradual move.

This (2000) is our best estimate as to when the title "liaison" was put into use at our library. There was an evolution from "selectors" with strictly internal collection development responsibilities to "liaisons" with outreach responsibilities over a period of several years.

This was following several years of pilots. Some subject-specific libraries offered liaison-style services to their disciplinary communities long before 2007. 2007 represents the date that system-wide liaison was implemented.

2010s

While many of the elements of liaison services were in place for decades, we began a review of professional librarian roles in 2010, and adopted a staff-generated proposal for restructuring using the liaison paradigm in 2012–2013.

4. **How were the liaison roles determined? Check all that apply.** N=67

Library administrative decision	56	84%
Library's perceived needs of a department(s) in the institution	48	73%
Informal conversations with members of the department(s)	26	39%
Formal meetings with department groups	18	27%
Surveyed members of the department(s)	8	12%
Other process	21	32%

Please briefly describe the other process. N=21

Again, this is a guess since I wasn't working here then.

Based on suggestions from a consulting agency, Booz, Allen, Hamilton, Inc.

Examining other liaison models and best practices.

Formal strategic planning, review of the literature, surveys to liaison librarians at other institutions.

Grew out of existing subject librarian roles and functions.

In some strategic areas, additional funding has been identified to hire a liaison librarian to meet specific needs (Executive MBA program and Sustainable Energy, Environment, and Economy).

It is difficult to confirm; so I am making an assumption.

Librarians approached the library administration about the need.

Librarians were tenured in the schools they served.

Library reorganization

More recently, liaison librarian roles are determined and assigned by branch heads, in consultation with the Libraries' Strategic Leadership Team, and roles are formalized for individual librarians through annual expectations.

Our model has been that every academic department has a liaison, though we have librarians who are liaison to multiple departments or schools.

Some disciplinary interests, as well as current positions, were considered, while this remained overall an administrative decision.

The original decisions that created the subject librarian role have been lost in the mists of time.

The review process was initiated in 2010 at the request of the dean of libraries. Professional librarians from across the university library were constituted as a task force to review the variety of services offered across the eight campus libraries, in the context of developing a broad paradigm of liaison services applicable across the diversity of subjects and schools.

This was so long ago, no one clearly remembers the exact process.

To the best of our knowledge this is how it was determined.

Unknown

Unknown how the service was established.

Unknown. We don't have any staff members that were here when the service was established to know the answer to this question.

Wow! Another good question! We should likely know this!

5. **Please briefly describe where liaisons are positioned in the organizational structure of the library.**
   N=65

Academic liaisons are positioned throughout the libraries system.

All liaisons report through to the same AUL, though they may have different direct reporting supervisors.

All library faculty (MLS) are liaisons. They all have departments assigned to them.

All members of the HSCL "reference and instruction" department (actually called Biomedical and Health Information Services; BHIS) are also liaison librarians. They report to the Head of BHIS/Associate Director of the HSCL.

All of the liaisons apart from the health sciences librarians are part of the Research and Information Services Division. Some are in special libraries. Most are in the main library, formerly in the Reference Department. We have recently reorganized reference into Research Services, Instructional Services, Online Services, Government Information & Data Services, and User Engagement departments, but almost all librarians in these departments have liaison duties.

All of the liaisons work in either the main library or one of the branch libraries. They are spread across both public and technical services areas.

All of the remaining science libraries are situated in the buildings where departments reside (Chemistry, Geology, PMA [Physics, Mathematics, Astronomy], Marine Science Library, etc.) The same is true for some of the arts and humanities, including the Classics Library, the Fine Arts Library, and the Architecture and Planning Library. Liaisons for the social sciences, some of the humanities, business, etc. reside in the main library, along with most of the liaisons to global studies/language departments.

All report to administrators (directors or associate university librarian), who are responsible for operations at the four universities.

As of 2015 they are distributed across three different library departments.

As of this writing, liaisons report through several different library departments and divisions. Liaison work is coordinated through a group of discipline-based coordinators. Three of four coordinators report through one department, Research & Information Services. One coordinator reports through the Branch & Off Campus Services Department.

At inception, liaison responsibilities were in the job description of each professional librarian. Currently, academic liaisons are primarily in the Research Librarians team, with other academic liaisons coming from the Global Resources Center and Special Collections. Liaisons to administrative departments may come from all parts of the library.

Department of Research and Scholarship, Special Collections Research Center, Learning Commons

Either the Reference Department or the Collection Development Department

In a separate department that also provides information services and general instruction. The department heads report to an AUL at several campus sites.

In Academic Affairs, liaisons are part of the following departments: Research & Instructional Services (formerly Reference and Global Resources & Area Studies, Music, Art, Stone Center, Sciences). In HSL, liaisons are part of User Services.

Liaison are within two divisions, Research & Education (R&E) and Special Collections & Area Studies (SCAS). Within R&E, liaisons are in Research Services, the Department Libraries and in Outreach & Engagement. In SCAS, there are Curators and Area Studies Librarians.

Liaison librarians are part of the Public Services Division.

Liaisons are currently positioned in the following departments: Collection Management, Research and Information Services, Centennial Campus Research Services; and the three branch libraries, Design, Natural Resources, and Veterinary Medicine. We are reexamining our organizational structure with respect to these roles/positions as we transform the roles of the disciplinary specialist librarians to involve deeper collaboration with researchers across the lifecycle of research, discovery, teaching/learning, and publication.

Liaisons are currently positioned primarily in subject-oriented departments. Before this structure, they were positioned all over the organization, and liaison roles were assigned solely on the ability to provide collection development, and not necessarily assigned to people who could fill all of the liaison responsibilities. Both faculty and staff in almost every department serve as liaisons.

Liaisons are decentralized and can be found all over our organizational chart. A majority come from Research & Learning Services, but there are other librarians from other departments who participate.

Liaisons are dispersed throughout departments within the organizational structure.

Liaisons are positioned primarily in the reference centers, institute libraries, and special collections, though some are located in service units such as Data Service.

Liaisons are situated within library units, often reporting to a unit head within the library. Liaisons take on one (or often more than one) subject area. We have also been experimenting with liaisons for other campus entities outside of academic departments (e.g., liaisons to the Office of Residential Life, First Year Experience, Undergraduate Research Centers, etc.)

Liaisons are tenure-track and non-tenure track faculty members.

Liaisons comprise one department and report to the Head of Research, Instruction & Outreach who reports to the Associate Dean for Outreach and Information Services.

Liaisons report indirectly through the Associate University Librarian, Research and Learning Services. Twelve of the liaisons report through four branch heads (who report to the AUL) and six liaisons report through the Head, Learner Support and Engagement Services (who reports to the AUL).

Liaisons report to department heads and directors of school and departmental units.

Liaisons report to divisional or department directors, which in turn report to the executive committee (UL and AULS).

Liaisons report to unit heads. While most liaisons have liaison work as their primary responsibility, some have a liaison role that is secondary to their primary role in other areas, for example, cataloguing, discovery, etc.

Librarians that serve as outreach, education, and/or selection for a subject discipline are liaisons.

Library faculty under disciplinary units

Most are within the same program area: Research Services. However, there are a few liaisons at regional campuses that have graduate programs. There are also a few liaisons who have been given smaller assignments based upon their expertise and interest.

Most of the liaisons are part of the Academic Liaison division, and are in one of three departments within that division: Research Services (70%), GIS and Data (10%), DC Regional Libraries (10%). The other 10% are part of Special Collections, which is part of the Scholarly Resources division.

Most liaison librarians hold primary responsibilities in other areas, with liaison as an add-on. Liaison librarians are coordinated by the Head, Faculty and Student Engagement, who ensures coverage of required areas.

Most liaison librarians report to department heads who report to the Associate University Librarian for Public Services.

Most subject librarian/liaisons are primary reports in the collections division, and report to one of five subject area coordinators (humanities, social sciences, sciences, health sciences, area studies) who report to an associate director. Liaisons with primary assignments in other areas typically have a secondary reporting relationship with one of the coordinators.

One to three levels down from the university librarian

Our subject liaisons are in public services.

Previously, they were all throughout the seven libraries, but because of the closure of one library and the shrinking/re-positioning of librarians, liaisons are now primarily in the Research Assistance & Instruction Department (formally Reference).

Primarily in the Collections, Research & Instruction department, but some liaisons are positioned in other departments.

Public services

Public services division

Public Services Division, front line staff

Report to heads of branch libraries, and in some cases, a supervisor under the branch head.

Scattered across the organization working collaboratively.

Subject Librarians, our liaisons, report to a subject team leader (Area Studies, Humanities, Science, Social Sciences) and live in the Services Division. The Services Division includes Collections, Outreach & Education, and Access (Circ., REF, ILL, etc.)

The Academic Liaison Program (ALP) Director reports directly to the AUL of Academic Services. The AUL reports directly to the UL. The ALP oversees the liaison work of all librarians; however not all liaisons report primarily to the ALP. All liaisons have similar core functions and duties, and some report to the ALP while others report to other service programs such as Collection Development and Management or Reference and Research Advisory Services.

The bulk of the liaisons (called "selectors") are in the Research Department; although we have many in Technical Services, Learning & Teaching, Health Sciences library, and Publishing.

The bulk of the liaisons report to University Libraries Associate Dean for User Services or the Assistant Dean for the Medical Sciences Library. Some area studies and language liaison duties are dispersed across other units.

The liaison librarians work in the Education and Outreach, Reference, and Collection Development departments.

The Liaison Services Department is in the Public Services division (reporting to AD for public services) and consists of both subject and functional (e.g., instruction, collections) specialists. It is co-managed by two department heads (Head of Liaison Services for Collections & Research Support and Head of Liaison Services for Instruction & Outreach). Branch libraries are not part of Liaison Services.

The liaisons report directly to the Team Leader for Research Services who reports to the Associate Director for Academic Engagement Services.

There is no linear reporting line but most are in areas focused on public services.

They are an extra-departmental team of faculty librarians with an elected chair and an advisory group of ex officio members.

They reside in departments such as reference as well as in area studies and specialized departments and there are a few in technical services areas.

They sit under the Information Services & Resources departments. These departments report to the Associate University Librarian, Information Resources & Academic Excellence.

Throughout the organization and across many of the departments

Two departments—Research and Instructional Services and Area and International Studies—are primarily comprised of liaisons. Both departments report to the AUL for Collections and Public Services. There are also liaisons in several branch libraries.

Typically liaison librarians report to the Campus Library director; some liaisons are not in a campus library, but report to the Director of Scholarly Communications, or the director of library digital services.

Under the Assistant Dean for Scholarly Communication and Collections in a group with collection development

Under the Associate Dean for Research and Learning Services, which also includes services for graduate and undergraduate students as separate but related areas.

When the program began, liaisons all had other responsibilities, which determined the reporting line and position in the library's organizational structure.

Within one of the main areas of the new reorganization called Academic Engagement, which consists of four teams. Liaisons are members of two of those teams.

Within public services mostly

Within the Research & Instruction Services division so they are all public services staff.

POLICIES AND OBJECTIVES

6. Does your library have a written definition/description of liaison service/practice? N=65

    Yes   47   72%
    No   18   28%

7. Does your library have written policies or guidelines governing the functions, activities, or responsibilities of library liaisons? N=64

    Yes   36   56%
    No   28   44%

8. Do liaisons participate in establishing policies governing their activities? N=66

    Yes   55   83%
    No   12   17%

    If yes, please explain their role in establishing policies. N=55

    A group of librarians participated in the negotiation of the 2007 liaison agreement. Subsequently, liaisons establish their annual goals and objectives for liaison with their immediate supervisor, along with other duties and responsibilities.

    Academic liaisons meet as a group to discuss various issues and activities. There is also a Collections Advisory Committee with representation from humanities, social sciences, health sciences, sciences, and fine arts.

    All members of Liaison Services participate in the annual planning process that develops departmental goals for the year. We also, as a department, review and revise our entire strategic document every two years.

    All our documents are designed with their input.

    All subject specialists meet twice monthly to discuss matters of mutual concern and approve changes in policies and procedures.

    As a group, the liaisons discuss and define best practices.

As expectations evolve, there is continuing discussion within the Collections division. As needed, the associate director makes statements of policy (especially for changes or in new areas). For several years, we have had a best practices-oriented meeting series (The Art of Liaison, Instruction, and Selection), which was initiated by one of our front line librarians: that series taps in-house expertise (and sometimes outside speakers), shares ideas, and builds consensus.

As library faculty members

Before 2014, we revised our guidelines document, in part because we were prompted and influenced by the New Roles for New Times: Transforming Liaison Roles in Research Libraries report by Jaguszewski & Williams (2013). Our revision process since then has been a group effort. A subject librarian steering group was created to work with the coordinator on establishing policies and plans for training.

Coordinator input was solicited in devising documents about liaison roles, and these documents were shared with liaisons for further comment before codification.

Determining best practices and setting general expectations

Each liaison, in conjunction with his or her supervisor, determines the various ways in which departmental or college-based assignment require their support (teaching, research consultation sessions, collection content development, outreach, special projects, etc.) There is no cookie-cutter approach.

Every few years, the documentation is reviewed by subject librarians and their team leaders via committee.

I'm not sure what you mean by "policies." Liaisons in the department participate in defining liaison activities.

In 2011, a task force with liaison participation created the document "Engaging with Library Users: Sharpening Our Vision as Subject Librarians for the Duke University Libraries." We also have template language pertaining to the roles of subject liaisons that are used to create liaison positions.

Liaison feedback is sought as policies are developed by the head of public services and the director of collection management.

Liaison librarians contributed to the creation of the core competencies document, and contribute in other ways on an as-needed basis.

Liaison representatives are members of two councils: User Services Council and Library Resources Council. Policies developed by councils are approved by the University Librarian's Cabinet, our senior management group.

Liaisons are consulted as colleagues in the establishment of policies.

Liaisons are dispersed throughout departments within the organizational structure.

Liaisons have various methods for serving their various disciplines. We have some core functions, but each liaison uses their own best judgment to serve their user groups.

Liaisons participate in planning activities and goals, and provide feedback on policies such as travel funding.

Liaisons share proposals in their home departments, with a library-wide liaison group that meets monthly, and with Leadership Council as appropriate.

Participating in review of literature, brainstorming sessions, composing and responding to draft policies.

Policy creation grows out of discussions, anecdotal evidence, etc. The details are specified in annual evaluation docs (annual assignment, goal and objectives, etc.)

Policy is not the way we would describe this but each liaison is trusted to identify the most needed services for the subject that they serve. There is a general or standard position description for public services librarians and the librarian develops a tailored position description in consultation and in agreement with their supervisor. They choose concepts from something like a menu of options and have the option to tailor the language further if needed and appropriate.

Provide feedback and other input as appropriate.

Steering committees are used in the department to guide activities and to provide assistance when needed.

Subject librarians were very involved in developing our overarching policy document, the Subject Librarian Framework (adapted from University of Minnesota's model).

Technically, the library does not have policies, but has established guidelines. The creation of guidelines is to some degree informed by the liaisons' interactions with patrons and programs. That is the level of their participation.

The department heads and Collections Coordinator seek input and guidance from the liaisons at regular meetings. The attached document is under review by the liaisons.

The following is a quote from the Library Liaison Group charge: "The Library Liaison Group (LLG) fosters coordinated communication among librarians with formal liaison responsibilities for the purpose of continually improving library services to campus departments and for nurturing collaborative activities between the library and other units on campus to strengthen the teaching, learning, and research experiences of faculty, staff, and students. To achieve this purpose, the LLG will: Establish general guidelines for the liaison program…."

The guidelines were established as the result of a task force, which was comprised of liaisons, and collected feedback from other liaisons.

The liaison librarians meet with their departmental colleagues, in groups called "Subject Teams" led by collection managers, and in two major divisional groups (Collections and Public Services), where they discuss practices, trends, and how to perform their roles and collaborate with faculty and students proactively and effectively in a changing environment.

The liaison program is being reconceived as part of a library-wide reorganization. The basic parameters are determined by the administration but liaisons are working as a team going forward to establish policies.

The liaisons are able to provide feedback on the basic liaison job description, and can offer suggestions for new directions for liaison work.

The Liaisons Team discusses and votes on any proposed changes.

The Librarian's Employment handbook is reviewed every five years by librarians and administrative representatives. They also participate in the development and revisions of the job description.

The policies are incorporated into our faculty guidelines. Through the faculty council process, academics contribute to the guidelines document and ratify the guidelines.

The umbrella description of the liaison librarian job description is broad; each liaison in discussion with their director will identify annual goals (typically in the annual performance review process) and priorities for the coming year. No liaison will emphasize ALL or even most of the designated functions and services as incorporated in the liaison document. Any system-wide revision of the liaison concept will be done in consultation with the liaison librarians.

Their department heads oversee liaison activities, and adjustments to policies are discussed in department meetings and in broader meetings of all library subject specialists.

There was a committee that fleshed out the guidelines and a number of liaisons where on that committee.

These are discussed at meetings of those concerned.

They are members of task forces, committees, etc. that review services and recommend changes.

They provide some input into their position descriptions, goals, and activities.

They were the authors of the policies.

They will serve on committees, task forces, or other work groups as appropriate.

Through committees and task forces, liaisons help shape their activities and policies. Divisional directors work closely with liaisons to determine the strategic directions for liaisons. 15 liaisons from the library recently participated in an ARL-sponsored institute at Cornell to discuss the future of liaisons. It inspired us to consider new directions.

Through discussion as a team. Note that activities may vary among liaisons dependent on the specific needs of their assigned units, as well as the willingness of the units to use liaison services.

Through individual decision making and group discussion. Policy establishment is usually a faculty-wide process, so they are discussed in either faculty meetings or collection and access meetings. Unanimity is uncommon, so while liaisons participate, they do not always get to decide how things will be. In cases where it's not up to the liaisons, the Scholarly Resource Development department usually makes the decisions, but it might be other groups as well. Liaisons have written goals and objectives, but they are not standardized across librarians.

Through the Library Engagement Team meetings (the name of our liaison program) and the Library Engagement Team Advisory Committee

We are conducting strategic planning activities and are discussing our draft liaison engagement guidelines that detail an annual plan to be created by each liaison detailing their goals for the year in specific areas such as instruction and outreach and how they related to the strategic plan. In addition, each liaison is responsible for documenting levels of engagement (# of instruction sessions, consultations, etc.) and their overall impact. We are still working on these documents so we're not able to share them but we hope to have them finalized by the end of 2015.

Weekly meetings to set goals, establish activities, assign duties, etc. These are then related to the strategic plan of the library. Ultimate responsibility for setting goals and policies resides with the Head of Clinical Services (our version of liaison services).

While the University Libraries does not have a policy governing liaison activities, it does have a Public Service Librarians Responsibilities Statement, which captures the various aspects of this role, including liaison. Librarians were involved in developing this statement, as they will be in its revision.

Yes and no. Librarian's are involved in their own reviews (through a peer review process) and are also involved in committee appointments that impact activities and (attempt) to set policies.

Yes through work on committees and that take place during regularly scheduled library-wide and subject librarian meetings

If no, please indicate who is responsible for establishing policies for liaison activities. N=9

Core liaison group, shared decision-making, library administration

In this context, I am not sure what 'policies' means. Each liaison is responsible for ongoing needs assessment of their constituency(ies) and determining what services and how to offer them. If the liaison wants advice, they have the resources of their manager, the liaison librarians group, and the User Services Department management team. Health sciences liaison services are highly customized to the particular user group environment and wants, and the expertise the liaison brings or develops.

No written policies

Policies for liaison activities are established by the Head of Reference in conjunction with the Associate Dean of Information Services.

Senior leadership, that is the Associate Directors and the Director, as well as department heads.

Supervisory staff

The director or department head

We have guidelines and as professionals, the liaisons determine what services they need to provide to their departments or colleges.

We have no formal policies.

We just have job descriptions—AD/Supervisors are responsible.

9. **Do liaisons have written goals and objectives (either personal or institutional) to guide their liaison activities?** N=65

Yes	42	65%
This is optional: some liaisons do, some don't	15	23%
Not yet, but we are planning to develop goals in the next 1–3 years	8	12%
No, and there is no plan to develop goals	0	0%

LIAISON RESPONSIBILITY ASSIGNMENT

10. **Please indicate which library staff categories have been assigned liaison responsibilities. Please make one selection in each row.** N=67

Staff Category	All	Some	None	N
Librarians	13	54	0	67
Other professionals	0	23	34	57
Support staff	0	12	43	55
Other staff category	0	7	40	47
Total Responses	13	56	45	67

If only some librarians are assigned liaison responsibility, please explain how they are selected. N=54

Based on position description and determined during the hiring process. Occasionally, liaison responsibilities are added based on expertise.

Based on position responsibilities, educational background, experience, expertise, and interest.

Currently, most catalogers are not assigned liaison duties, though some of them do share public services responsibilities and DO have liaison roles. Some systems librarians do not have liaison roles. Some librarians with administrative responsibilities may not have liaison roles.

Designated as subject specialists: the liaison role is inherent in the job duties.

Faculty librarians with subject responsibilities are automatically considered liaisons. Not all faculty librarians have subject responsibilities. And not all of our liaisons have MLS.

For academic liaisons, those with collecting and teaching responsibilities are selected.

Hired specifically for that job. On occasion they may be assigned as needed, or as responsibilities move around with faculty (library) changes.

I believe that most librarians have some sort of liaison role, but hesitate to say that all do. As mentioned previously, some are liaisons to academic departments, others are liaisons for other aspects of the university, including campus initiatives, academic support, etc.

If they have any responsibility for providing outreach to students and faculty and they do some kind of instruction, then they are considered liaisons.

In general, librarians not in Technical Services, User Experience, IT, Admin, and Special Collections.

It is based on subject expertise, educational experience, and role within the library. A final decision is made by the liaison coordinator and the Associate Dean of Collection Development and Access.

Liaison librarians are selected through a formal open search process. In other words, they are hired into the positions.

Liaison responsibilities are most commonly assigned to subject specialist librarians, but expertise can determine that another professional may take on such a role.

Liaison responsibility usually accompanies job duties as a collection manager, research/reference librarian, or branch librarian. Currently, our Digital Library Initiatives department houses one liaison who specializes in digital humanities and visualization services.

Liaison roles are assigned as part of specific jobs with job descriptions. For the most part, librarians are hired into these positions.

Liaisons are librarians with direct contact with academic departments so this does not include technical services or access services staff.

Liaisons are primarily based in public service units.

Liaisons are selected based on their expertise and interest in subject areas.

Liaisons have been selected and hired for liaison responsibilities based mostly on their subject knowledge or work experience in a particular field.

Librarians are assigned according to their academic background, interests, department, and ability to serve all the needs of the departments.

Librarians are hired for liaison roles in the main library and several branches, but there are also many non-liaison positions filled by librarians.

Librarians are hired into liaison roles based on the subject or functional needs at the time. We have other librarians who are hired into collections support and systems positions who do not have liaison responsibilities.

Librarians engaged with reference, research support, and instruction also have responsibility as liaisons. This is described in job descriptions and recruitment materials.

Librarians who do not work in public service related positions are not necessarily assigned liaison roles. Several catalog librarians have liaison roles but most do not.

Librarians with primary assignments in technical services (acquisitions, cataloging), systems and web services are less likely to have liaison duties (but a few do).

Librarians within technical services or IT focused departments (among others) are no longer tasked with public liaison roles. Liaison assignments are primarily based on formal position descriptions that note liaison work as a primary activity and often denote what department/area the librarian will liaise to. This change reflects an increased specialization of roles within the research library.

Many are selected by virtue of background or subject expertise. We are branching out to include functional expertise as well, for example, copyright, metadata, images, electronic resources, etc.

Members of the Research and Information Services division, including specialized libraries. We have assigned liaison duties only to public service librarians.

Most have these in their job description. A few with functional librarian responsibilities (such as cataloging) have volunteered to liaise to a department of interest.

Most were selected in 2007. As staff leave, we seek others to replace them from around the library. Most liaisons hold either collections, area studies, or public service functions. Most functional specialists do not also hold specific liaison appointments.

Only librarians in the department of Information Services are assigned liaison responsibility.

Only the subject area librarians are liaisons.

Public services faculty librarians have liaison duties in job descriptions.

Public services librarians in reference departments have liaison responsibilities.

Reference & Instruction librarians have liaison responsibilities in their job description. Librarians in other departments volunteer to take on liaison responsibilities.

Research support librarians have a primary role of liaising with faculty and students. Tech services and library IT librarians are not assigned these roles.

Responsibilities and qualifications for liaison services are included in job posting.

Selected based on subject expertise or academic degree, previous liaison experience, or department need.

Selection is based on subject expertise and interest on the part of the librarian.

Self-selection as part of the reorganization. Some were assigned to cover gaps, particularly in the sciences and engineering.

The liaison program grew out of the reference program in the 1980s, which had subject expertise as a hiring factor. Now we hire based upon knowledge, expertise, and skills currently needed.

The majority of librarians with liaison responsibilities have them as part of their broader public services portfolio. However, there are also librarians who have liaison responsibilities who work in other areas. They are often selected based on language abilities, subject background, experience, interest, etc.

The majority of the librarians are subject specialists or liaisons. Those who have this responsibility are typically hired with some set of skills or requirements that match the needs of that department/school/discipline, etc. However, we have many librarians who have no formal background in the areas they serve. For example, we have social scientists who serve science disciplines.

They are all subject/reference librarians.

They are hired as liaisons (or subject specialists), or they had the liaison function in their job prior to the establishment of the Academic Liaison Program reorganization.

They are hired into a liaison role as the subject librarian or curator. Other librarians are hired as technical services librarians or functional specialists. Upon the retirement of a subject librarian, subject areas may get reassigned to other subject librarians, area studies librarians, or curators or we may re-hire in those same subjects.

They are in outward-facing research support roles or have language proficiency that correlates with an area of study. Most liaisons are in the User Services division; a few are in the Technical Services division (which includes Collections & Licensing as well as Cataloging & Metadata Services). ·

They are selected based on their association with academic departments, which is informed by either their bibliographer responsibilities or reference/information services responsibilities.

Those librarians that serve a subject discipline are liaisons. They may be a liaison to a department or a college.

Those with a workplan of greater than 50% designated to support clinical services have the title clinical services librarian. All reference librarians must do some clinical services but their level of effort is less than 50%. Librarians in collections, historical archives, and administration may not have any clinical services responsibilities.

Usually those with subject expertise.

We have specific liaison librarian positions that librarians are hired into. We have other librarian positions such as cataloguers or the digital repository librarian, which don't have liaison responsibilities.

We hire and appoint for specific subject areas. Each vacant position is reviewed by the library faculty and relevant administrators for continuation or adjustment.

We may start using a professional as well who has an MLS.

Answered "All Librarians" N=5

All members of the information services/collections departments at each campus site serve as liaisons. There is also one professional in another department who serves as a liaison, and the plan in the coming year is to incorporate at least one more person outside the department.

All reference librarians and bibliographers have liaison duties.

Liaisons are only in the department formerly known as Reference.

Most of our subject librarians are considered professional librarians (MLIS or PHD in subject area); a few with language specialty are liaisons without above.

We hire directly for liaison positions; liaison duties are included in their job descriptions.

If other library professionals are assigned liaison responsibility, please list their position title(s).
N=19

Archivist, Bioinformationist: Biomedical Sciences Liaison

Chinese Studies Specialist

Curator

Director of Communications and Outreach, Director of Scholarly Technology, Executive Director of Development, Finance Director, University Human Resources Client Partner

Diversity intern

GIS analyst: outreach for GIS and related services

Government Information Specialist. Other professionals might include our OEPs and temps, who often fill in for liaison responsibilities.

In 2001, some catalogers and bibliographers were given liaison responsibilities. Now everyone is called a "subject librarian" who has this role.

Instruction Librarian (formerly had not specific departmental subject liaison roles—that has since changed. But in the initial formulation, this is one position that led to the realization that there were staff with liaison roles who were not 'subject liaisons'. GIS Coordinator is another—also a professional position that is not a 'librarian' position. Head of Access Services—another professional position, not classified as librarian. Institutional Repository Coordinator. Director of Scholarly Communication.

Learning librarians, accessibility librarian, visualization librarian, GIS Librarian, Student Enrichment & Community Outreach librarian, Video Game Archives librarian, instructional technology librarians, publishing outreach librarian, Informationists (Medical librarians)

Library manager: professional staff

Other library professionals are assigned liaison responsibilities based on their functional, as opposed to subject, expertise. One example is our Data Library Coordinator.

Polar Curator, Ohio Congressional Curator

Programs and planning department has liaison relationships. These include grants, programs, communications and programming professionals.

The ALP has high-level library assistants who have advanced degrees in relevant subject areas, serving some of the functions of a liaison librarian.

To be determined

Varies

We are increasingly hiring liaisons without library degrees but with deep subject knowledge. We have hired three recent PhD students to each division—science, social science, and humanities—to liaise with faculty and students in areas of digital humanities, data management, and other aspects of the research lifecycle.

We have an archivist who oversees the Canadian Architectural Archives, who has an MLIS.

If support staff are assigned liaison responsibility, please list their position title(s). N=12

At HSL, interested support staff have been assigned a back-up or assistant liaison role. Their position titles have not been changed but their job responsibilities have been adjusted.

Cartographic & Geospatial specialist: outreach for GIS and related services

Library Assistant

Library Specialist, Sr.

Programs and planning department has liaison relationships these include grants, programs, communications and programming staff. Events staff has liaisons relationships as well.

Senior Library Technician

Support staff are not usually assigned exclusive liaison responsibilities, but are assigned supporting responsibilities, such as bibliographer's assistant, or helping with teaching.

The ALP has an Outreach Coordinator staff position responsible for event planning and management. This position does not perform liaison duties directly, but indirectly serves and facilitates one of the primary functions of the liaison program.

To be determined

We have a few language experts (Dutch & Scandinavian) who serve as liaison librarians. They are part of technical services and not research.

We have one library assistant IV, whose position is in technical services and supports cataloging in Asian languages, who has functioned as the 'subject liaison' for Asian and Chinese studies. For many of the faculty in her area, she functions and is considered by them fully their liaison librarian. The formal role of Asian Studies Liaison is held by a professional librarian, but for CJK materials s/he defers completely to this person. The LA IV is currently in an MLIS program and will get the degree within a year.

We have two support staff who were hired in the 1970s when a deep subject knowledge without a library degree was enough to be hired into a librarian position (one has a deep understanding of the performing arts and the other has a subject Master's). 1. Library Coordinator, Chinese Language/Literature, East Asian Languages & Literatures, Germanic Languages & Literatures, Holocaust Studies, Japanese Language & Literature. 2. Subject Specialist for Art, Dance, Drama, Film, Visual & Performing Arts

If another category of staff is assigned liaison responsibility, please describe that category. N=5

At HSL, Research Assistants (first and second year library school students who are employed half-time by HSL) gradually take on some liaison responsibilities in a back-up or assistant liaison role. These responsibilities can include staffing office hours in another building, team teaching or solo teaching within the curriculum, helping with consults and reference inquiries for a constituent group, or creating subject guides for a particular group.

Other staff help with some collection management related duties, primarily support with foreign language materials.

The library has a number of people who are IT professionals who do a great deal of liaison work—but they are not assigned to any particular discipline or academic department. These include the manager of the 3D lab, academic technologists, and manager of emerging technologies.

Varies

We have one case where a professional librarian who served in a liaison capacity was allowed to go part-time. At our university, we have no part-time faculty so the position was changed to staff. The position retained its liaison title. This is the only case of a non-professional position used for liaison work.

11. Please indicate how many positions in each staff category have liaison responsibilities. N=63

Staff Category	Minimum	Maximum	Mean	Median	Std Dev	N
Librarians	6	110	29.49	26.00	18.18	63
Other professionals	1	10	2.81	2.00	2.18	21
Support staff	1	5	1.80	1.50	1.23	10
Other staff category	1	5	2.75	2.50	1.71	4

12. Please rate how important each of the following qualifications is for selecting liaisons at your institution using a scale of 1 to 5, where 1 = Not at all important and 5 = Very important. N=66

Qualifications	1 Not at all important	2	3 Moderately important	4	5 Very important	N
MLS (from an accredited school)	0	1	10	10	44	65
Second master's degree	2	12	30	17	4	65
Relevant undergraduate major	1	6	36	17	6	66
Scholarly research/publication	8	22	23	11	2	66
Minimum 1–5 years' experience	6	23	18	14	3	64
Participation in professional associations	7	16	26	10	6	65
Language expertise	13	10	22	14	6	65
Demonstrated communication skills	0	3	4	19	40	66
Other qualification	4	1	5	8	17	35
Total Responses	27	44	63	51	61	66

Please specify the other qualification. N=30

5 Very Important N=17

Ability to work on a team and collaborate. Technology skills and knowledge are increasingly important.

An understanding and interest in the subject matter.

Collaboration/teamwork skills

Collaborative, entrepreneurial, innovative

Collegiality

Commitment to liaison work, interest, good instruction-related skills, comfort with and interest in fund management.

Curiosity, interest in new technologies

Customer service/user-centered focus

Demonstrated willingness to experiment and learn about users' needs, perspectives, and preferences.

Enjoys getting into the work and meeting environments of users; demonstrated initiative and innovation; technologically skilled and adept at learning new technologies, subjects, and approaches; team oriented and proactive in sharing what is learned.

Experience teaching, experience with collection/content development, research consultation/reference experience, etc.

Knowledge of health sciences clinical resources. Knowledge of health sciences curriculum and accreditation trends.

Project management skills, instruction/teaching skills, collection development & curation skills

Skills or aptitudes for data analysis and visualization, data management, and the use of tools and technologies that support and enhance research and scholarship.

Teaching experience

Teaching skills

Technical abilities, as applicable to the specific subject/liaison duties. Familiarity with scholarly communication issues.

4 N=8

A terminal degree related to their area of liaison responsibility; technical training

Experience in outreach and instruction; technology skills

Experience with instruction; experience with another functional area (for example, data management)

For some very demanding subject areas, expertise like GIS background, some foreign languages, etc. are required.

Personal interest or affinity; good interpersonal skills; ability to meet the needs of the respective constituency

Project-specific needs

Research and Learning Services Librarians are all expected to have a liaison role.

Subject expertise—doesn't have to be a master's or PhD

3 Moderately Important N=5

Depends on the specific position and the subject specialty assigned.

GIS and/or data for certain positions, outreach and marketing

Informal connections to other campus units (such as past work history or personal interest) sometimes lead to liaison connections. Interest or expertise in emerging areas such as data management or digital humanities/text mining can bring value in some subject areas.

Subject expertise (PhD or job experience), awareness of digital scholarship, demonstrates teamwork, collaboration, and engagement

Willingness to participate in the liaison program

Comments N=24

Although we hire liaison librarians without an MLS, the hires are required to obtain the MLS within a 3-year period as part of our continuing faculty status process.

Depending on the specific liaison responsibility, the qualifications may become more or less important.

For language expertise, it depends on responsibilities, but if language expertise is needed for the position, then it is very important.

Importance of qualifications is dependent on the type of position being filled.

It depends on the discipline. For instance, if they are the liaison to the French department, they most likely speak French.

It very much depends on the needs/specialties of the department to which the librarian will be serving as a liaison. We have liaisons without an MLS but with other special qualifications, we have librarians with second master's and PhDs, and we have librarians who are liaison because they have good communications skills and are comfortable as a liaison for a department in which they don't have an academic specialty.

Language expertise is critical for area studies liaisons.

Language expertise is critical for international and area studies librarians, but not as important for other liaisons.

Language expertise is important for area studies (international studies) and selection in areas where non-English language materials are important. Participation in professional associations covers groups such as Medical Libraries Association or SALALM. We do not expect librarians to attend annual meetings such as the American Historical Association (although some do, on occasion).

Language expertise is important for some disciplines, less so for others.

Language expertise is required for those in area studies, but would not be a requirement of others (although certainly a plus). Experience is also a plus but we are happy to hire entry-level people who demonstrate excellent communication skills, ideas about and understanding of liaison work, and indicators of potential success. We expect all librarians to be involved in professional associations and scholarly research; but the expectations depend on the level of the librarian.

Level of importance could vary with position. If the person is the Middle East Studies librarian, for example, then language knowledge is required.

MLS is preferred, but not required for librarian positions. Librarians are expected to have the ability to engage with faculty and students, and perform the functions required of the position.

Our library does not require a second master's degree and few librarians have one, but for those who do it does factor in to department assignments. The same is true for language expertise. It's uncommon and unnecessary in most cases, but we do take advantage of those skills when available in assigning appropriate departmental responsibilities.

Scholarly research/publication and participation in professional associations are expectations of liaisons but not required pre-appointment qualifications.

Some liaisons are responsible only for collections; others have areas which are liaison-only. Number of staff above excludes one liaison who is a collections librarian only. Some liaisons are curators of special and specialized collections.

Subject expertise, communication skills, and the ability to collaborate are the highest qualifications.

The ability to work with a group of diverse colleagues is important, as is the ability to work independently achieving the goals of the department.

The majority of our librarians have limited disciplinary expertise in their liaison roles, with most holding disciplinary degrees in English or History.

The ranking above reflects an overview of liaison service positions. These may change in importance depending on the specific subject area. An example is language skills needed for specific subjects.

This question is ambiguous as to whether it is an entry level or experienced and very discipline specific. Another qualification could be projecting confidence.

Undergraduate degrees are considered when appointing liaisons, especially when they do not have a second master's degree. For 2–3 liaison roles, language expertise is very important for selection (e.g., Humanities Subject Librarian).

Whether or not the MLS or second master's degree is important depends on the liaison assignment. For the bioinformatics position, MLS is not required but advanced science degree is.

While a second master's degree or relevant undergraduate degree can absolutely contribute to the success of a liaison's role, we have traditionally hired for relevant library experience and excellent soft skills, which are essential for effective liaison.

13. **Please indicate whether liaison activities are a primary or secondary responsibility for each staff category. Please make one selection in each row. N=65**

Staff Category	Primary	Secondary	Not applicable	N
Librarians	61	4	0	65
Other professionals	8	12	37	57
Support staff	5	4	43	52
Other staff category	1	4	42	47
Total responses	61	18	46	65

Comments N=28

As noted above, liaison is a primary responsibility for most librarians who have it, but is indeed secondary for some.

Few liaisons have ONLY liaison responsibilities. Most balance liaison responsibilities with other duties.

For 26 of our liaison librarians, liaison work is their primary activity. Two liaison librarians split their assignments between liaison work and cataloging.

For librarians in subject specific campus libraries (e.g., education, art, chemistry, etc.) liaison is a primary responsibility. For those in general libraries, liaison is in most cases a secondary responsibility.

For most librarians who are liaisons, it is a primary responsibility, but for a few it is a secondary role.

For the 30 librarians and 2 staff identified as liaisons, being a liaison is their primary responsibility.

For the few librarians with smaller liaison assignments (e.g., Head of Cataloging as liaison to Judaic Studies), the liaison responsibility is secondary.

For the librarians in question (liaisons), their liaisons activities are their primary responsibility.

I chose primary; but this is very individual—for some it is primary, for some secondary. No one is just a liaison.

It is a primary responsibility for librarians who are liaisons, but not for other librarians, as those who work in technical and automated services.

Liaison activities are also secondary for some librarians, depending on how many subjects they are covering and how much work those subject are. Also, not all librarians are liaisons, so for some, it's not a responsibility at all. For support staff especially, it's usually only a very small part of their job to provide liaison support.

Liaison activities are primary for most librarians who do liaison activities, but secondary to a few with functional responsibilities.

Liaison activities are the primary responsibility of subject specialists in our Liaison Services Department.

Liaison activities connect with all core responsibilities, such as reference, collection development, and instruction, so in that sense it is primary.

Liaisons activities are only primary responsibilities for public service librarians. About 2/3 of our librarians have liaison roles.

Most liaison librarians have this work as a primary assignment, but some assist with liaison coverage on a secondary assignment basis (we lack enough librarians to cover all areas as thoroughly as we might wish).

Not all faculty librarians are liaisons. Above table is applicable only to liaison librarians.

Note that for the archivist, liaison responsibilities are a secondary role. However, will be a primary role for the bioinformationist.

Primary for the subject liaisons

Some librarians have liaison work as their primary responsibility, while others do not, so it is not really possible to answer this category accurately. See comment regarding portfolios, above. Also, in the case of Other Staff, those who work with liaisons do so in the capacity of assisting informally, rather than have this as a primary, or even secondary, responsibility.

The allocation of liaison responsibilities varies from position to position.

The core liaison activities of outreach and collection development are generally secondary responsibilities for all librarians. The additional services of instruction, reference assistance, and research consultations are primary responsibilities of Reference & Instruction librarians, based on their job descriptions.

These answers apply only to the subject specialists. We have many librarians and staff who have no responsibility for liaison activities, e.g., metadata or acquisitions people, and those in management positions.

This question is ambiguous. Liaison activities are the primary responsibility for the librarians and staff assigned those duties, but not for others.

This varies by liaison and/or discipline. For most, liaison activities are a primary responsibility, but for some it is secondary or lower.

This varies by position description, not by type of position.

Though we have many who are liaison librarians in a secondary role, we do have librarians whose primary role is as a liaison. Librarians whose primary role is as a liaison work in generally large colleges/departments with extensive acquisitions budgets and demand for services.

Varies among individuals.

LIAISON'S DEPARTMENT ASSIGNMENT

14. How are a liaison's department assignment(s) determined? Check all that apply. N=67

Based on liaison's subject expertise	65	97%
Based on liaison's position	45	67%
Liaison self-selects the department(s)	20	30%
Distributed to equalize the ratio of faculty/researchers to liaisons	18	27%
Liaison follows an application process	6	9%
Other criteria	20	30%

Please specify the other criteria. N=20

Ability to build relationships with students and faculty in their assigned subject areas.

Affinity to other assignments

All appointments as liaisons, however they are initially suggested, are approved by the head of Scholarly Resource Development department, the director of the relevant subject department, and the liaison's direct supervisor.

Background and workload considered in new liaison assignments.

Based on institutional need to cover what needs to be covered.

Based on the needs of the library and departments.

Either where gaps are identified or new programs are initiated.

Informal conversation leads to a decision by the department head.

It is also historical assignment & random as people leave the organization.

Liaison is interested in learning a new area. Liaisons have sometimes chosen areas for these relationships.

Liaisons are hired to fill specific departmental roles, but these shift with staff changes and all of the other factors listed may come into play in making those assignments. The non-liaison responsibilities of liaison librarians are also weighed in balancing responsibilities. Equalizing is not strictly a matter of faculty/researcher ratios as different departments have different needs in terms of instruction, collection development, etc.

May be based on need or availability, or the fit with other job duties.

Occasionally need-based, due to attrition.

Organizational history, established relationships.

Primarily, we recruit for a specific liaison position. Some liaisons have been willing to commit time and training to learning a new subject area, e.g., the Clinical Services Liaison has spent up to 25% time learning new clinical domains in order to expand services to new hospital departments.

Some assignments reflect the need for coverage, as best we can. Coordinators often cover when other librarians are not available.

Subject specialist may negotiate with their colleagues and director if a balance in workload or change in subject focus arises.

Those items checked off MAY figure into the determination of role, but frequently the assignment is determined by individual capacity or interest.

Usually, these are determined within the context of the liaison's unit in relation to their academic background, workload, responsibilities of other liaisons, etc.

What we need to cover.

15. Is a liaison assigned one or more than one department? N=67

Some liaisons are assigned only one department; some are assigned more than one	50	75%
All liaisons are assigned more than one department	17	25%
All liaisons are assigned only one department	0	0%

If liaisons are assigned more than one department, please indicate the minimum number and maximum number of departments that are assigned to any one liaison. N=60

Number of Departments	Low	High	Mean	Median	Std Dev	N
Minimum	1	4	1.35	1.00	0.73	60
Maximum	3	100	9.43	7.00	12.64	60

16. Does the library assign a liaison to every academic/research department or only to some? N=67

Every department	59	88%
Only some departments	8	12%

If only to some departments, how are those chosen? N=8

Most departments have a liaison, but in cases where we don't have enough people, the liaison role might be grouped under a larger level organization (such as a liaison to the College of Music instead of individual departments). The campus has numerous centers and organizations that could use a liaison but we don't have a system for identifying those, though we are working on them.

Newer departments that tend to be highly interdisciplinary and pull instructors from other departments, such as the honors college, do not have a liaison; rather, they tend to be served by several librarians, depending upon subject expertise needed.

The intention is to cover all departments. With staff turnover there are times some departments are not covered or we lack anyone with any relevant skills to support them. New programs and new departments sometimes have arisen and it may be a few years before we were able to define someone to cover them.

The liaison assignments are based on historical need. Some are affiliated with departments, some by faculty (professional faculties in particular), and some by discipline or interdisciplinary unit.

They are chosen based on enrollment in the department and the department's importance to the university.

This is a good question. I think most of these decisions are made at the unit level, and seem to be based on a mix of tradition/relationships and emerging campus needs.

This really depends on how you define departments. Some liaisons are assigned to schools within the university that may consist of multiple departments. That would also change the answer to some of the questions above.

Those that express an interest in clinical services support; those that actively include clinical services support in curriculum or research agenda.

Additional Comments N=7

Every department is the goal, but we sometimes discover gaps, new needs, etc., and we assign liaisons whose subject expertise best matches the need. We do have some departments who have not responded to outreach and therefore require only minimal contact with a liaison. There is no minimum or maximum number of assigned departments. At this time, we see little correlation between the size of a department and the workload of the liaison. Assessment is needed in this area.

Every department on paper, but in practice only some are active departments.

HSL does not assign by departments. We have liaisons for schools (School of Dentistry) and programs/research areas (bioinformatics, translational science, cancer information).

Some liaisons are assigned a college rather than individual departments. The liaisons assigned an entire college may work as a team.

Some liaisons serve an entire college such as education, nursing, pharmacy, medicine, dentistry, medicine. Some colleges have two liaisons such as engineering and business. Other liaisons serve one or a two departments or programs.

The university has numerous institutes where we may not have an identified liaison, e.g., life sciences institute and data science institute are two examples.

We have attempted to assign a liaison to every department, however this is now proving unsustainable, and many departments in medicine no longer have a direct disciplinary liaison. In addition to departments, we have assigned liaisons to some centres, institutes, and areas of study that fall outside of departmental areas.

17. Which members of the department are eligible for liaison services? Check all that apply. N=66

Teaching/research faculty	66	100%
Other faculty (adjunct, term, non-tenure track, lecturer, etc.)	65	99%
Graduate teaching assistants	63	96%
Graduate students	63	96%
Undergraduate students	62	94%
Administrative staff	58	88%
Other category	15	23%

Please specify the other category. N=15

A health sciences center has different categories. Too many to list here.

All members of the university community are eligible for liaison services.

Alumni, retired faculty

Anyone else involved in department.

Community members whose interests fall into one of the subject specialties. At HSL, anyone affiliated with a school or program area is eligible for liaison services, including community groups engaged with them. Depending on the level of involvement of the liaison, a fee for service or grant funding might be proposed.

Fellows, visiting professors, etc.

Members of the public, too, as part of our land-grant mission.

Officially, our liaison program is a faculty liaison program. However, many liaison librarians voluntarily offer services to graduate students as time permits.

Professional students (medical, dental, vet med, nursing, public health and health professions, pharmacy); post-doctoral associates; clinical residents; clinicians

Research staff and the public (we are a land grant), non-administrative staff, anyone

Researchers, other affiliates, and potential students

University administrators/officers, visiting scholars, researchers, post doctorates, and those working as part of a grant-sponsored organization.

University staff. Liaisons also assist community members with research and provide library instruction to visiting external groups such as area high school students.

Visiting researchers and scholars

Visiting scholars, researchers, etc.

18. **Does the library assign a liaison to administrative support departments, such as an Office of Undergraduate Research or Student Affairs?** N=65

Yes, to all departments	1	2%
Yes, to some departments	38	59%
No, only to academic/research departments	26	40%

If you responded "yes to some," please list the departments that are assigned a library liaison. N=36

Academic computing offices in the schools, Office of the Dean in each of the schools

Ag Extension

Athletics, Career Center, International House, Writing Studio

Athletics, Division of Research, Writing Center, Learning Support Services, Student Affairs, Faculty Development & Instructional Services, Graduate School

Career Center, Center for Teaching Development, Teaching and Learning Commons, Technology Transfer, Undergraduate and Graduate Student Affairs, Research Affairs, Diversity, International Center, and more. Current relationships have developed over time based on individual liaison decisions. This is another area where assessment is needed.

Center for Teaching & Faculty Development, deans of the schools and colleges, the Writing Program, Disability Services, Continuing & Professional Education. We are beginning to look at assignments for the support departments listed in the question above.

Columbia College, College of General Studies, College of Engineering, The Writing Center, centers and institutes across the university

Depends on whether their potential use of the library and/or possible need to do research.

Division of IT, Vice President for Research, Undergraduate Research Center for Student Engagement, International Student Services, Undergraduate and Graduate Student Admissions, Academic Technologies, Disabled Student Services, Online Education, University Teaching and Learning Center, University Writing Center

Educational technology, the international student center, disability services, the student success center, office of entrepreneurship, online education, digital humanities center, LGBTQ center and Women's Center

First Year Experience, Student Affairs, Office of Research, Technology Enhanced Learning (division of Information Technology)

GE in the curriculum, institutional research, president's office, alumni office, Center for Teaching & Learning, Center for Scholarly Technology

Graduate Division, Graduate Resource Center, Student Outreach & Retention Center, Office of Access and Inclusion, International Center, Division of Undergraduate Studies, Transfer Student Center

Honors College, Global Scholar's Hall

Honors College, Grad School, undergrad research program

Honors, First Year Initiatives, TRIO

Key research centers, Office of Diversity & Inclusion, Alumni Office, First-Year Experience

Liaisons are assigned informally to administrative support units. These include student support services such as: Student Accessibility Services, the Native Center, the Student Success Centre, and the Institute for Teaching and Learning.

Liaisons are assigned to institutes within the university. All liaisons provide services to administration and other areas of the university.

Liaisons or the head of a unit may serve on a committee such as undergraduate student success, graduate student success, medical education, etc.

Office of Undergraduate Research, New Student and Family Programs, Office of Fellowships, Undergraduate Admissions, Norris University Center, AccessibleNU, Counseling & Psychological Services (CAPS), Center for Student Involvement (CSI), Northwestern Career Advancement, Residential Academic Initiatives, Study Abroad, Student Enrichment Services, NU Athletics, The Writing Place, SustainNU

OGAPS (Office of Graduate and Professional Students, which includes the Thesis Office), University Writing Center, International Student Services, English Language Institute, Center for Teaching Excellence, Honors and Undergraduate Research, Student Affairs. NOTE: This list is growing as we identify core partners where we can make the most impact in supporting teaching and learning activities on campus.

President's Office, Office of Academic Affairs

School/college-based: Art or Design installations (VPA, Arts & Sciences), Honors Program, English Language Institute (University College), Maxwell Executive Education Programs (with Librarian for Communications, Public Administration, Political Science & International Relations). Academic (non-school/college-based) and Administrative: Academic Integrity Office, Athletics, International Students (Slutzker Center for International Services), Office of Multicultural Affairs, Office of Residence Life, Parent's Office, Posse Program, SU Abroad, SU Sustainability Division, Transfer Students, Tutoring & Study Center, University College Veterans

Some liaison assignments are at the college level (including multiple departments and other units such as a veterinary hospital). Examples of other offices/centers/institutes on campus include: Graduate School; Research Support Council; Center for Geospatial Analytics; Center for Innovation Management Studies; Office of International Students; Student Support Services; Undergraduate Tutorial Services/Writing & Speaking Tutorial Services; New Student Programs.

Study Abroad, Fulbright, various programs

This is underway; likely departments include the writing center, student affairs, financial aid.

This question is unclear. One of our liaisons is to the CTSA (translational science) central program on campus and serves those who elect to be members (free) of the program. One of our librarians is a Personal Librarian for approximately 30 transfer students as part of a program the University Libraries runs with several campus administrative offices. One liaison has the hospital department managers group and the quality improvement group as assignments. Another librarian has developed a liaison relationship with a research administrators network, representing several 100 research study coordinators and research assistants across campus. At University Library: Undergraduate Research, First-Year Writing, National Resource Centers are a few examples.

Too complicated to list, selected case by case.

Units with a recurring need for library liaison include those dealing with freshman composition, English as a second language, LBGTQ services, international studies and programs, and the resource center for persons with disabilities.

University College, Writing Center, Tutoring Center, Graduate College

We cannot give details at this time since this is a new initiative.

We do increasingly assign a liaison to specific administrative departments, such as our Centre for Teaching and Learning, Undergraduate Research Initiative, Faculty of Graduate Studies and Research, Aboriginal Student Services Centre, Student Accessibility Services, etc.

We have informal relationships with the following: The Graduate School, Office of Distance Learning, and Office of Research.

We have librarians who liaise with undergraduate research program but we don't have one for the graduate college, for example.

We have programs and centers and other offices (such as undergraduate research office) that have liaisons.

Additional Comments N=4

The Head of Faculty and Student Engagement acts as liaison to division-level and on direction to VP-level offices, in close consultation with the AULs, deputy chief, and chief librarian.

Formally, we do not have liaisons to administrative departments. We have liaisons who link to a number of them and essentially provide support, but our designated liaison roles are only to academic departments.

Our Outreach and Education team does liaison with many administrative support offices, such as Office of Undergraduate Research, Office of Undergraduate Teaching, Writing Center, Office of International Students, etc., but it is not part of the formal subject librarian program.

We do work with other departments across campus, although we do not have specific liaisons designated to these departments.

DEPARTMENT PARTICIPATION

19. Do all of the departments with a liaison take advantage of the services provided by library liaisons?
N=66

Yes   38   58%
No   28   42%

If no, please estimate the percentage of academic/research and administrative support departments that actively participate in the library liaison activities and describe which departments those are. N=24

Academic/research departments

66

30%, Writing & Rhetoric, History, School of Medicine, School of Nursing, School of Professional Development, Health Technology & Management, Dental Medicine, Social Welfare, Psychology, Journalism, Asian & Asian American Studies, Business, Intensive English Center

35%

40–50% English, social work, some engineering, some business, linguistics, communications, psychology, anthropology

40%

60%; health & exercise science; biology; aerospace & mechanical engineering; civil engineering & environmental science; electrical engineering; geography; African-American studies; history of science; geology & geophysics; international & area studies; political science; anthropology; religion; philosophy; history; math; physics & astronomy; classics; film & video studies; modern languages; art; music; architecture; social work; education

65% or more

66%

75%

80%

85%

90%

95%

98% Too many to list.

99% All academic departments participate in the liaison services in some way, but the extent of participation varies.

All liaisons have consultations but it would be difficult to estimate the percentage of outreach efforts to which departments respond.

Almost all departments are active, difficult to estimate the number which are not, as we have not done a quantitative study.

Difficult to determine since most participation is at the individual faculty level rather than the department.

It is easier to describe which departments are not actively taking advantage of liaison services, e.g., computer science.

This is not easily quantified. Approximately 75% of academic/research departments use liaison services, but within those, usage varies widely by individual faculty.

Uncertain even to estimate.

Unknown; for example, the Computer Science Department does not actively seek out or engage in regular interaction with their liaison, although the liaison works on collection building and other important internal support functions.

Unsure

Varies over time.

Administrative support departments

100

1–5%

10%

50%

75%

Honors, First Year Initiatives, TRIO

I am not able to estimate this one.

N/A or 10%

Uncertain even to estimate.

Undergraduate Colleges, Educational Opportunity Program,

We need to identify which departments we have not reached. All those with whom we work have been open to collaboration on a variety of things.

20. Is your library actively seeking ways to increase participation from departments? N=67

Yes	64	96%
Not yet, but we plan to	3	4%
No	0	0%

If yes, what methods do you use? Check all that apply. N=64

Encourage liaisons to attend department meetings	63	98%
Market liaison services	62	97%
Other method	50	78%

Please briefly describe the other method. N=49

Annual meeting with departmental faculty liaisons

Any method of engagement that is appropriate for the respective department.

Anything and everything we can think of. Evolving every day. Classes, mailings, events, press releases, cooperative programming, on-site embedded activities, teaching and collaborative teaching, shared positions, affiliate faculty status within a department, etc.

At HSL, liaisons choose methods for their schools and programs. Most provide regular/annual reports about their services to key administrative contacts. HSL regularly publishes success stories on its news page and "I Love My HSL blog", in annual reports, and other venues. The director and liaison meet annually, jointly, with health affairs deans, hospital administrators, CTSA Program Director, and others with whom we have liaison personnel assigned.

Attend campus events.

Attend new faculty orientation, attend dissertation defenses and other departmental events, provide departmental orientations, attend subject-specific conferences (e.g., Modern Language Association)

Blogs, newsletters, office hours, research projects

Calling for faculty to deposit documents into the Institutional Repository; consulting on data management plans

Co-authoring papers and presentations; locating grant opportunities; consultation on content mining, data visualization, and use of Libraries' visualization spaces and displays; assistance with finding and acquiring spatial and numeric data; consultation on using GIS and online mapping software; participation in classes (sometimes) as a mock "client" for student projects; serving as final reviewers for student projects; consultation on biosketches and other components of grant proposals; support for information management and citation management. Librarians attend seminars with clients to build relationships and extend availability for informal questions.

Collaborative teaching and learning experiences. Collaborative projects such as teaching classes in the library with a librarian actively participating in the class instruction.

Constant outreach on behalf of the liaison

Embedded librarians, library publications, formal and informal meeting opportunities with prospects

Embedding liaisons in places such as the Writing Center, attending talks and presentations in departments, partnering with divisional deans on outreach, doing CV reviews for faculty to include items in our institutional repository, hiring graduate students as interns to spread the word about library services and collections in their departments, support faculty digital projects and digital humanities initiatives.

Encourage and promote liaison collaborations and outreach of all varieties, including department events, orientations, embedded services, etc.

Engaging in research data management activities across campus will be one way for us to promote library services to students and researchers.

Enrolling in courses through canvas

Faculty interviews to determine their research needs, departmental visits to explain new services available, formal training program to provide outreach, instructional and content knowledge support

Implement a customer relationship management system for contact management and building a knowledge base of user needs.

Individual contact with dean, unit director, faculty or administrative staff

It is hard as we are very low staffed, but we try to do as much outreach as possible.

Make individual contacts and meeting with new faculty.

Meet outside the library; attend department events

New services, liaisons to research centers and non-academic departments, disciplinary faculty on library committees

Newsletters, office hours, a variety of techniques varying according to the nature of the departments and programs

Offer new services where liaison assistance is valued.

Office hours in academic department; involvement of department in recruitment & hiring of librarians; service on department committees, invitations to library events

Office hours in departments, support departmental events on occasion, attend theses defenses, participate in department committees such as curriculum committees

One-on-one conversations to determine departmental needs and how the library can position itself to fulfill them

One-on-one meetings, especially with new faculty

Outreach (attend department events, participate in campus activities, etc.)

Participate in departments' activities, such as conferences, work one-on-one with faculty on projects, like setting up exhibits or working on joint publications, serving on committees in the departments and campus, etc.

Participation in a variety of campus outreach events such as new faculty orientation.

Recent feedback from the Ithaka Faculty Survey indicated that some faculty are not aware of some of the liaison services we provide. We do plan to do more to promote these services in response to faculty feedback. We work closely with our university Grant Assist Program to promote some of our liaison services, like scholarly communication support, research impact and data management workshops, etc.

Reference assistants are trained to refer walk-in patrons to subject specialists and provide business cards, which are also on display in the reference area.

Regular communication via multiple channels (emails, newsletters, etc.)

Regular communication with faculty, orientation sessions for newly hired faculty, orientation sessions for new graduate students and teaching assistants

Requesting faculty include contact information for librarian on syllabi.

Serve on committees of the health-related colleges and departments (such as curriculum committees, accreditation committees, writing support groups, search committees, etc.) To better reach students, we perform outreach through

National Library of Medicine exhibits and extensive event/speaker series to complement them; have faculty from academic departments serve on library faculty search committees.

Social media, office hours, workshops, campus partnerships

Study curriculum and research-intensive courses to target those, infuse library into campus-wide undergraduate research initiative, present at new faculty orientation and new student orientations

Support research and grant projects

There is never 100% for any service offered. That is unrealistic and it is a moving target as to the participation since it may depend on faculty and classes.

Training for "elevator encounter," attending morning report and rounds. Sponsoring journal clubs and others.

We are currently planning an examination of our outward-facing activities, which will help us identify new methods.

We are investigating how to become more involved in research support for scholars. There are a number of initiatives underway that will draw on greater scholar participation in liaison activities.

We are looking at workload to try to free liaisons to spend more time with people in their assigned departments and to develop and promote new services.

We have recently undertaken an external review with participation from over 50 university leaders across the institution, as a way to better understand needs, create awareness, and engage the community.

We plan to provide group training.

Working collaboratively to spend allotted collection development funds, electronic newsletters and informational emails, targeted workshops for faculty or for staff, etc.

LIAISON SERVICES

21. **Please identify the core duties of liaisons at your library. Check all that apply.** N=67

Providing one-on-one research consultations	66	99%
Managing library collections in disciplinary areas	65	97%
Outreach and communicating news and items of interest from the library	65	97%
Teaching one-shot information literacy sessions	64	96%
Providing consulting on scholarly communication issues	55	82%
Reporting news from disciplinary departments to the library	53	79%
Embedding in discipline-based courses	51	76%
Providing data management consulting	42	63%
Regularly staffing the reference desk	41	61%
Teaching semester-long research or information literacy courses	28	42%
Other duty	31	46%

Please specify the other duty. N=31

Assisting teaching faculty to identify library resources and services for the courses and assignments.

Bioinformatics support; clinical rounding services; mediated literature searching; providing assistance with/co-authorship on systematic reviews; creating and teaching credit-bearing courses, such as "Human Bioinformatics" or credit-bearing honors college courses related to National Library of Medicine exhibits; organizing and implementing center or institute seminar series or annual conferences; teaching workshops on the NIH Public Access Policy compliance, medical terminology, bioinformatics resources, and best practices in data management.

Co-hosting of events & programs at library

Community outreach and education to various constituents

Connecting to functional specialists, connecting to other relevant liaisons

Creating online subject guides. Providing support for citation analysis for faculty evaluation, promotion. Participation in library and campus committees.

Creating research guides and support materials

Cultivating subject and interdisciplinary knowledge, keeping abreast of new technologies

Data research and identification, office hours, virtual reference, LibGuides

Digital scholarship, impact metrics

Event planning is not necessarily a core duty but is expected from the group of liaisons as a whole. A few have taught semester-long research or IL classes but it's not a core duty. Liaisons collaborate with other our data curation program on data management consultations.

Liaison's role in managing library collection is changing as we change our print/electronic collections management processes. While most of our liaison are no longer staffing the reference desk, there are some small branches where this is still a core role.

Liaisons are the initial point of contact for faculty seeking library services. Some liaisons provide teaching of IL classes; others collaborate with reference and instruction librarians to provide these services.

New competencies added as a result of 2014 revision: Knowledge and advocacy for the use of digital tools (e.g., Zotero, DMP tool, etc.)

Not all liaisons do all of these but they have access to other librarians to whom they can refer. Most are involved in teaching, consulting on, and doing systematic reviews and other extensive research work. Some liaisons are learning basics of data management planning, data visualization, data repositories, and related support. They all help users with compliance with public access policies from research agencies. They all help users set up research alert services and dynamic embedded searches of resources like PubMed and the catalog. All provide expertise in presenting professionally from poster critique to finding publishing venues (including open access) and we have an instructional design specialist for consults regarding working with images, poster creation, visual literacy, and similar concepts. Finding grant funding, teaching, and helping faculty, staff, and students use the funding sources tools is another popular service. I know I'm forgetting others!

NOTE: Our institution does not offer semester/quarter-long information literacy courses.

One liaison teaches a semester-long IL course related to her department, but this is not the norm.

Our Science & Engineering Library has on-call reference support; they do not staff that desk.

Participation in curriculum planning, grand rounds, morning report, journal club, systematic reviews, etc.

Providing digital scholarship support. Support for using and manipulating certain formats, such as visualization data, maps & GIS

Providing direction to Digital Scholarship Team

Purchase of software to support faculty and student research needs. Training on software. We regularly staff our digital centers with librarians doing research support, but we no longer have any reference desks in our libraries.

Refer for assistance on data management and copyright/open access. Develop integrated information literacy programs for their department rather than only one shots. Providing information on new library services, new collections, etc. Having office hours in the departments. Providing assistance with bibliographic management software, etc.

Referring users to data management and scholarly communications staff for consultations; course design; technical computing support

Research & research grant support (literature search, systematic reviews, co-PIs), assignment creation & marking, academic integrity, some supervise library associates, lead committees and projects

"Staffing the reference desk" includes the online and virtual aspects of our "Ask Us" service such as providing help and consultation via chat and text messaging. Also, liaisons introduce faculty and students to "the library as a research platform," including technology-enabled spaces for visualization, digital media creation, and interactive computing, along with tools for data analysis, visualization, and management.

Teaching 0–1 credit subject-specific information literacy courses

Text and data mining, and research data management advice, for campus units in which there is interest.

Walk-in and virtual reference (We do not have a reference desk.)

We no longer have a true reference desk, but we do staff a research consult desk.

Working on data management skills and some embedding

22. **What is included on the menu of services that liaisons offer to their assigned department(s)? Check all that apply.** N=66

Departmental outreach (updating departments on new library services, resources, etc.)	66	100%
Reference assistance	66	100%
Communicating departmental needs to library	65	99%
One-shot instruction	65	99%
Collection development	64	97%
Integrating library instruction into the curriculum through collaboration with faculty	63	96%
Scholarly communication education	59	89%
Assistance with scholarly impact and metrics	58	88%
Promotion of institutional repository	55	83%
Consultation on open access issues	54	82%
Creating web-based learning objects	53	80%
E-research support	53	80%
Data management support	52	79%
Consultation on intellectual property issues	47	71%

New literacies education	38	58%
Other service	16	24%

Please specify the other service. N=16

Data visualization support, GIS support

Facilitate partnerships within the library and across campus for research and digital scholarship initiatives.

Integration of special collections objects into curriculum, partner on digital research projects

Literature searching, support for systematic reviews

New faculty orientation to the library (consultations), large orientations for new undergrads and grads (N.B. not all liaisons do all things on this list.)

Not all liaisons provide all of these services. They may put a faculty member in their department in touch with the IR coordinator for repository questions. Consultation about IP is becoming a much larger role and we are ramping up training so all liaisons will be comfortable responding to these, though can also refer complex issues to Director of Scholarly Communications.

NOTE: library instruction is not part of our curriculum per se, but we conduct instructions sessions for specific classes. We do not have an institutional repository.

Program partnerships, e.g., exhibits, panel presentations

Promoting Digital Research Services. At HSL, collection development is not a primary role of HSL liaisons. Typically, the liaison works with the HSL Collections Development Librarian or turns over requests to that librarian. For new programs starting up, the liaison will work with the Collection Development Librarian to assess the collection and access needs and help determine appropriate resources with the faculty involved. Liaisons are often on program teams in the schools preparing and participating in program reviews and accreditations. Often the liaison is asked to draft the library or information competency related portions of documentation for these. We also have access to a University Library Scholarly Communications Officer for complex intellectual property, copyright, and fair use questions. Liaisons know the basics. We promote the liaisons as a "face" to HSL for any questions, resources, or services they need and the liaison is equipped to handle, refer, advocate, or discover what will meet the user's need.

Promotion of open access journal development, provide e-theses deposit support for institutional repository

Referral services to different libraries, service units, and functional specialists

Text mining, for units with interest. For consultation on copyright and intellectual property issues, a liaison librarian may play a role in referring library users to other library staff.

The other non-checked items we refer or work at different levels.

We have an IP (intellectual property) expert in the library who handles these requests. Liaisons are generally aware of the issues but not experts in IP.

We offer a workshop series on research topics: literature review, ORCID, altmetrics, impact factors, EndNote/Zotero, etc. Creating LibGuides for subject areas and for specific courses.

Working with departments on development of student exhibitions. This role, along with others listed, is dependent on departmental interest and uptake.

23. **How do liaisons inform departments of services that they can offer? Check all that apply.** N=66

Send information via e-mail	65	99%
Meet with faculty individually	65	99%
Attend departmental meetings	63	96%
New faculty orientation	62	94%
News on library's homepage	59	89%
Promotional flyers, brochures, etc. sent to department	44	67%
Special events such as technology fairs	44	67%
Promotional flyers, brochures, etc. in library	40	61%
Blogs	36	55%
Library newsletter	35	53%
Electronic discussion lists	33	50%
Ads or articles in campus newspaper	21	32%
Other method	21	32%

Please briefly describe the other method. N=21

Announcements in weekly campus news service email

Annual reception for new faculty and departmental representatives

Attend faculty retreats and strategic planning sessions, send messages for distribution by administrative staff, electronic information boards in buildings, office hours on site, attend or participate in faculty or student research days, membership on curriculum and technology committees, etc. Not all methods used by all, as stated previously. There is also value in relationships and visibility built over time. While we have had turnover in liaisons, a fairly stable faculty come to know, rely on, and seek out the new individual in the liaison role.

Campus magazine and library magazine

During summer orientation, the library's services and resources are included in students' materials, as well as during the parent orientation session focusing on academic resources.

Grad student orientation, screen savers, book marks, posters highlighting subject librarians

Informal coffee, random meetings on campus and beyond

Liaisons increasingly work with campus partners to insert information about liaison services into departmental print/ electronic newsletters, and to promote relevant workshops, etc.

LibGuides

Mass-marketing (mail chimp), social media, attendance at social & cultural events

Referrals from questions received by the general email and instant messaging reference service.

Social media (2 responses)

Social media. We are very environmentally conscientious and are trying to minimize paper trail as much as possible, thus we try not to send any paper products to departments, including flyers, brochures, etc.

Some use social media.

Special events include presence at various "fairs" hosted by other groups on campus, as well as orientations at the beginning of the academic year.

Student orientations, departmental student organizations

University staff newspaper, all-faculty monthly newsletter sent out by VP that may include 1–2 short items from the library

Various methods depending on nature of department or program

We don't have many actively blogging, and those who do I have no way of knowing what faculty read them. We do have twitter posts, and many of our news online pieces go there as well; some make it to the university news online.

We have very limited access to marketing help.

24. **Please identify additional partners with which liaisons at your institution typically work. Check all that apply.** N=61

Center for teaching and learning	54	89%
Information technology	45	74%
Student affairs	41	67%
Office for institutional research	39	64%
Office of accessibility	35	57%
Office of sponsored programs	34	56%
Office of assessment	27	44%
Other partner	28	46%

Please specify the other partner. N=28

ACCAD Advanced Computing Center for the Arts and Design, Centers like ME Center, Center for Medieval Renaissance Studies

Advanced research computing, ICPSR, medical school

Digital Humanities Center, VP for Research

Distance Education and Learning Technology Applications (DELTA)

First Year Experience, Residence Life

General education program

Informatics (different than information technology), Graduate College

International Programs, Honor Council, Center for Multicultural Equity and Access

Interprofessional Education, college-level curriculum committees and accreditation committees, individual research and clinical faculty, National Medical Student Association

Library administration liaises with Office of Research, Athletics, etc.

Library has its own IT department, liaisons with specialization in RDM connect with Office of Research

MITH (Maryland Institute for Technology in the Humanities), graduate studies, honors programs, undergraduate college

None of the above

Office for international studies and programs: liaisons in area studies are especially engaged here.

Program for Instructional Excellence (PIE offers training for teaching assistants), Office of Distance Learning, and the Graduate School

Program for Writing and Rhetoric

Residence Life, Graduate School, various research institutes, interdisciplinary cross-departmental/cross-campus initiatives

Some liaisons have appointments as fellows of the university's undergraduate residential colleges. A few liaisons have adjunct appointments with the academic departments they serve.

Special Collections, Digital Scholarship Center, Writing Center, and the campus museum

Student Success Center (tutors, career center, writing center), Provost's Office, Office of Sponsored Programs, Census Data Research Center, Admissions

The Graduate School and student organizations, for example the Graduate and Professional Student Federation have been partners on specific events.

Undergraduate Research Initiative, Aboriginal Student Services Centre, Grant Assist Program offices, etc.

University Foundation

University Housing, First Year Programs

University Writing Center, Office of Thesis

Writing center

Writing Center, Learning Support Services, Athletics, Graduate School

Writing Center, Tutoring, international student organizations

25. What methods, direct or indirect, do liaisons use to assess the needs of faculty, researchers, students in their liaison departments? N=65

Communication (conversation, email, etc.) with faculty, researchers, students	65	100%
Documentation from departments, such as strategic plans, promotion and tenure guidelines, and handbooks	49	75%
Surveys to faculty, researchers, students	47	72%
Other method	28	43%

Please briefly describe the other method. N=28

A couple of liaisons have undertaken projects to interview faculty and graduate students in departments.

All forms of personal and formal communication are used.

Bibliometrics analysis (some library faculty do this)

Communication with students (during workshops, reference, consultations)

Curriculum review and mapping, student and faculty advisory boards

Curriculum review in which there is an assessment of each department's student learning outcomes and syllabi.

Focus groups, Town Halls on specific issues

Focus groups, accreditation studies, feedback/comment board

Gen Ed requirements, major requirements, course syllabi

Grant awards, program reviews, and curriculum and course changes

It has been several years since we've done any formal assessment. Most of it is word-of-mouth.

Liaisons wrote and continue to update environmental scans of their subject areas. These scans are shared within the library as liaisons share trends they discover during this process. Liaisons share their scan with their subject areas to open dialogue and to verify the results of their update.

LibQUAL+®

Libraries are required to supply a report for each new programs proposal. Some other PCC materials are also read by liaisons as they become available.

Library instruction and consultation statistics

Office of Sponsored Programs highlights grant documentation, course offerings, citation and publishing trends, seminar papers.

Participation in university-wide activities, service on university committees, attendance at outside events. We also received information from the college of arts & sciences on curriculum changes.

Review of curricular materials, ethnographic research, focus groups, usability testing

Review of faculty vitae and documented research interests.

Reviewing of departmental and major student learning outcomes, course syllabi

Surveys are used infrequently and selectively for high priority issues. Asking participants questions before and after instructional sessions is fairly common. Other documentation includes survey results from those the schools and programs conduct, as well as website reviews, research awards announcements, and the meetings with deans and key administrators mentioned earlier.

Syllabi and assignments provided for instruction sessions, research consultations, and reference work.

University strategic plan

University strategic plan, presentations and emails from the provost

We also look at number of classes, learning objects requested, and the amount of students who make use of those things.

We have recently used focus groups for our "Future of the Libraries" report. Focus groups are used irregularly, typically when we have a conjunction of several issues we can present and request input about.

We track how many classes and consultations occur, and how many students and faculty are served by our services.

Working on joint scholarship or projects.

26. Does your library support collaborative, team-based problem solving through its liaison program?
N=64

Yes, we encourage liaisons to share expertise in order to solve problems collaboratively	62	97%
Not yet, but we are planning to start encouraging this sort of work in the next 1–3 years	2	3%
No, there is no structure in place to support collaborative liaison work	0	0%

Comments N=10

Along with evidence-based practice support

Department meetings offer a forum for liaisons to discuss issues and hear feedback from colleagues on how to best address a situation. These conversations are always interesting and productive as the group shares their experiences.

Increasingly, we see faculty needs that benefit from expertise coming from different parts of the library: subject specialists, data and text specialists, copyright specialists, GIS specialists, and so on. This leads to three-way conversations: researcher, traditional liaison librarian, other specialist.

Not sure what this is referring to. Our liaisons collaborate with one another to solve problems, etc. and share solutions.

Our organizational structure brings subject and functional specialists together in a single department, and these librarians collaborate in nearly all their work.

Representative liaisons manage collection development via subject teams. Liaisons with the same subject responsibilities work across universities. Representative liaisons meet monthly as members of the User Services Council, Library Resources Council, and the Committee on Scholarly Communication.

Structure for this is emerging. We are intentionally trying to create conversation and collaborative units NOT structured around campus library staffing but rather around disciplinary clusters across libraries.

We create cross-functional project-based teams.

We have journal clubs for liaisons on topics such as education and we have liaison gatherings such as pizza parties and picnics.

Yes, we are doing this, but in an unstructured and not robust manner.

CHANGES TO LIAISON SERVICES

27. Has the liaison role at your library undergone recent changes? N=67

Yes, we have recently incorporated changes into our liaison roles	49	73%
Not yet, but we are currently planning changes to our liaison roles	12	18%
No, and there are no plans to incorporate any changes	6	9%

If yes or you are planning changes, please briefly describe the most significant changes to liaison roles and responsibilities. N=56

Added consultation for scholarly impacts, open access, intellectual property issues, and support of institutional repository.

Addition of collection development responsibilities. Reduced emphasis on one-shot instruction. Increased emphasis on consulting with faculty to create library-focused assignments.

All liaison work is now the sole responsibility of library faculty. We no longer have non-library faculty (professional staff) handling any liaison work. And all library faculty are now expected to be liaisons, in theory. Previously, only some librarians were liaisons.

Closing the reference desk freed up some time to focus on more concentrated marketing of liaison efforts. We are also trying to get more up to speed on IP/copyright and open access issues. This fall we will be promoting our new IR.

Cutting back on reference desk hours, establishing undergrad services unit to handle most undergrad instruction, encouraging stronger relationship development with academic departments, scholarly communication

Data management has been added to liaison responsibilities. There is an increasing emphasis on outreach. We are planning to lessen reference responsibilities to focus more on instruction, consultation, and online interactions.

Data management has recently been incorporated.

Data management tools, open access education and support, increased marketing of services through the E-Research and Digital Scholarship Services unit.

Development of Subject Librarian Framework in 2010

Due to a total overhaul of our organization, our subject librarian structure has been rethought and re-imagined this past year. We are only beginning to implement the new structure in the fall where collections duties are separated from research and instruction duties. Instead of one person handling all assigned duties for an academic department, a team of librarians will be taking on different aspects while staying in close communication with each other.

Expanded with evolving scholarly communication roles.

Expanding standardized efforts, collaboration on course and assignment development

I think these things are changing, but I have not yet seen evidence of organization-wide conversations about this.

I'm not sure what you mean by recent. Yes and no. Liaison roles have not changed significantly in the past several years. At HSL, as our users' needs evolve, liaison roles are changed. For example, with 2008 NIH public access policy implementation, all liaisons began to help researchers and others comply. As global health emerged as a university priority, liaisons developed their knowledge of users' needs and resources available to support them, whether library-based or otherwise. As data management has emerged as a need, liaisons develop their knowledge base to enable them to meet those needs. As researchers used the library facility less, liaisons became increasingly present in the locations that researchers and their students are working. Liaison roles, services, and knowledge are continuously evolving.

In 2014, the Libraries developed a set of core competencies for liaisons and guidelines for completing annual work-plans and year-end assessments. Self-assessment is a big part of this evaluation process that concentrates on impact of each activity.

In the last year we've reorganized our reference department in order to provide more focus and support. We are still working on clarifying the roles and expectations of liaisons and more actively promoting our services.

Increased emphasis on collaborative relationships and engaged services over one-shots and collection development

Liaisons are distributed among three different library divisions. We're dividing some duties by functional expertise or subject expertise. Liaisons were not distributed among different departments prior to 2014.

Liaisons are expected to provide support for data management, use of the library's high-tech spaces, and visualization. They develop and promote our digital collections resources to facilitate new modes of research and support sophisticated research using the library's spaces, including large-scale visualization labs, and technologies. Connect clients with potential collaborators, both in the Libraries and throughout the university.

Liaisons serve on our Scholarly Communications Committee. Liaison members of this committee train other liaisons in issues related to the IR, scholarly communications, and data management.

Liaisons will be trained to assist faculty with the new open access university policy that goes into effect September 1, 2015. Assistance with data deposits is in the future.

Major change was that role was expanded to include core competency development in scholarly communication, digital tools, and data research services, including development of data management plans. Another change is using "functional specialists" to consult with liaisons on various projects (e.g., assessment or data services librarians who are also liaisons).

Merged Collection Development department with Research & Instruction department, and now called Collections, Research & Instruction department. Development of core competencies document. Development of liaison librarian best practices document is in progress.

More emphasis on research consultation with students and faculty. Collaboration with other units in library for digital scholarship services and data management. More emphasis on integrating library instruction efforts to curriculum.

More team approaches, expectation to be able to advise researchers about topics such as data management (advice is not the same as performing data management functions: in most cases, our goal is to identify referrals).

One recent change, based on customer input, we changed our name from "Subject Liaison" to "Subject Librarian." Added "keeping abreast of new technology." Added "cultivating interdisciplinary knowledge." Added more assessment.

Over the past couple of years, scholarly communication, research data management, and research impact have been incorporated into the liaison librarian role. With this, there has also been a significant amount of staff development and training to support folks in taking on these new roles. While not every liaison takes on these roles to the same degree, each is developing their expertise to be able to offer these new services as requested.

Reference desk duties, embedded librarianship

Research data management and scholarly communication are new areas of responsibility when communicating with faculty, researchers, and students.

Simple review of existing services, for example, we now offer data management services, which is new since our liaison program framework was written.

Subject specialists have given up review of approval books in order to have more time for liaison and teaching.

The addition of new functional specialists (e.g., Instruction Design Librarian and Social Science Data Librarian) has expanded our liaison offerings to include new services.

The major shift was with the 2012–13 report and paradigm adoption. Evolution and refinement of the paradigm is continuing.

The mission of the library focuses on providing individualized service. Liaisons are referred to as Personal Librarians to reflect this emphasis.

The most significant recent change is taking on collections responsibilities, which had been handled by bibliographers in a separate department.

The project-based teams are a new structure.

There's been a shift from a collections-centric to engagement-centric model. We are continuing the development of liaison roles at the point of contact for connecting users with specialized staff and services related to digital scholarship, data and visualization, scholarly communication, etc.

Using a customer relationship management system to document and manage user contacts.

We are currently seeking to hire a new director for liaison services at the main library. With new leadership the liaison role will evolve and improve.

We are in the process of reviewing the model of liaison services.

We are planning to review our program for currency, and to promote more outward-facing engagement and less direct work with collection development. Part of this effort will involve examining our support for new and emerging academic areas on campus. Additionally, our library is undergoing administrative restructuring, and as a result we will see differences in roles and reporting structures. One other change, which has been in place for about a year, is reduced number of hours at the general reference desk for liaisons.

We are rolling our research data management services where liaisons, primarily subject experts, will liaise with departments in new ways.

We are trying to grow in data management and scholarly communication support.

We are trying to increase the role liaisons play in scholarly communication issues.

We began doing much of our work in "working groups," and liaisons participate in those groups with significant contributions. Instruction and reference consultation are now expected of all liaisons, where before it was considered optional.

We focus much more on scholarly communication issues and data management than we have in the past. This varies across disciplines, with more data management in the sciences and social sciences. The turn to digital humanities has created new opportunities for humanities librarians. All liaisons have become more involved in our institutional repository by communicating with faculty and students about the repository and doing CV reviews to add more material to the repository.

We have added specializations.

We have been moving towards a model of more externally focused engagement, less emphasis on collection building, increased emphasis on research support.

We have incorporated not only "subject" based liaisons (for example, pharmacy, veterinary medicine), but also "functional" liaisons, that cut across disciplines, such as consumer health, clinical and translational research, bioinformatics (and the soon to be advertised health literacy).

We have lost access to a lot of our technology support so are trying to develop more technology skills in liaisons' positions/new hires.

We have recently included scholarly communication and additional options for determining metrics/impacts, and are working to expand knowledge of and incorporation of open access/open agenda, data management, etc.

We have undertaken a year-long assessment of our liaison program, including liaison librarian and faculty focus groups, and an external review. We are now moving forward to engage with our community to review and adopt these recommendations.

We revised the basic liaison job description to make it more engagement focused, and also developed functional teams. We are working on the team contracts and competencies for those functional teams.

We will be developing expectations for our liaisons around support for scholars, scholarly communication, and data management.

We adopted the Engaged Librarian Framework in 2011.

Yes, we recently expanded beyond traditional, subject-based role to an "engagement team" to include functional specialists who are essential to the Libraries' information literacy role as well as capturing, curating, and preserving campus scholarly output.

28. What were the primary factors that led to making these changes? Check all that apply. N=61

Changing landscape of scholarship and publishing	50	82%
Identification of new needs within the university or parent organization	42	69%
New leadership within the library	32	53%
Changes to the university or parent organization's strategic plan and goals	25	41%
The addition of new roles or responsibilities within the university or parent organization for library liaisons	17	28%
New leadership within the university or parent organization	11	18%
Other factor	24	39%

Please specify the other factors that led to making changes in liaison roles and responsibilities. N=24

A wave of retirements within the library offered an opportunity to consider new directions and organization.

Another catalyst, mentioned earlier, is the New Roles for New Times report published by ARL.

As liaisons learn about emerging priorities or new programs within their assigned areas, they share that knowledge and work together with library managers to determine how to address those.

Changes in the disciplines, changes in accreditation standards, changes in the curriculum

Changing landscape around research services, e.g., GIS and data management

Creation of learning commons

Desire to expand library's role in teaching, research, and scholarship. Also the scope of liaison work is too broad for one person to do everything. We have distributed some of the functions across different people.

Federal government regulations for making data publicly accessible

Group's self-identification of new roles and the desire to document subject librarians current work.

Growth in online learning (at World Campus and all the campuses across the state), improvement in communication infrastructure to support scholarship and learning

Increased workload and reduction in support staff have created an increase in workload. Liaison librarians need a new vision for the future in order to prioritize their goals and activities, and determine where reskilling is needed.

Library reorganization

Need to make library faculty role more prominent/relevant to academic missions of university.

New administrative library structure was put in place to eliminate redundant activities.

New librarian hires

Opening a new, 21st-century library designed to be a technology-rich "research platform"

Organizational changes within the library, which included the merger of two subject librarian/liaison discipline groups (Science/Engineering and Humanities/Social Sciences/Education) and the posting for a new director to serve over the newly merged units.

Reduced staffing

Significant areas of liaison were not working well, inhibiting our understanding of faculty needs and requirements that were changing rapidly.

The "subject" model alone did not address known and emerging gaps in information needs.

This change was made by the current Head of Research, Instruction & Outreach to better reflect the role of the liaison to faculty and students.

To refine and better articulate the program and address issues such as annual reporting, training, outreach, and marketing. To improve skills and abilities of liaison librarians.

Tri-Agency Open Access Policy on Publications, CIHR research data policy

We had been organically changing how we deliver services so it was time to formalize those changes.

29. Who was involved in making the decision to change liaison responsibilities? Check all that apply.
N=61

Library administrators	59	97%
Supervisors to library liaisons	54	89%
Library liaisons	47	77%
Other, non-library organizational administrators	7	12%
Other participant	8	13%

Please specify the other participant in the decision making process. N=8

A committee participated in creating the liaison program, including the Scholarly Communications Librarian and others who envisioned working with the liaisons to accomplish their area's goals.

All staff

By liaisons and HSCL leadership serving on committees and partnering with groups in the Health Science Center, we were able to keep abreast of changes in missions, goals, academic programs, etc. that required the addition of "functional" liaisons to meet info needs.

Constituent groups being served

Disciplinary coordinators/consultative role

Each of these new areas tended to have one or more "champions" among front line liaison librarians, who were seeing campus needs and became knowledgeable about options.

It is evolving naturally. Recent job descriptions have been updated to reflect these changes.

The decision was made partly based on input from a library-wide strategic planning process.

30. Have liaisons at your library relinquished any responsibilities in order to integrate new ones? N=64

Yes, liaisons have shifted responsibilities	38	59%
Not yet, but there is a plan for this sort of shift in responsibilities to happen over the next 1–3 years	16	25%
No, there is no plan for liaisons to shift any responsibility	10	16%

If yes or you are planning this sort of shift, please briefly describe which liaison roles and responsibilities have shifted. N=46

As a result of more targeted collection development and patron driven acquisition, some liaisons will be shifting away from collections work. There will also be greater emphasis put on scholar support rather than on in-person general library instruction.

Collection development

Collection development responsibilities for liaisons have changed somewhat with the advent of shelf-ready and patron driven acquisitions. Liaisons still select materials but not to the extent that they once did.

Decrease in desk responsibilities and decrease in first-year instruction

Decreasing reference desk hours, decreasing undergraduate instruction responsibilities

Depending on workloads, some work fewer or more hours on general reference or instruction.

Eliminate reference desk responsibilities.

General reduction in in-house reference services, less emphasis on collection development duties, many fewer formal classes offered

In general, liaisons are doing less collections work. And we are revamping our instructional program to shift responsibility for information literacy in introductory courses to a small team of teaching librarians, rather than the liaisons. This frees up the liaisons to concentrate on integrating research methods into upper level and graduate level courses, and to work on curriculum mapping to identify other areas for interactions.

In recent years, we have gone to shelf-ready aggressively, reducing the need to review physical books as we have in the past. In general, we focus more on services and less on collections than we have in previous years.

It is underway, but our biggest challenge has been getting staff to identify and relinquish responsibilities.

Less focus on references, more PDA in collection development freeing up time for deeper liaison connections with departments in other ways.

Less focus on selection and more focus on education, support, and collaboration.

Less front-line service, less item-by-item selection of materials, more focus on data consultation services when appropriate to research needs.

Liaison librarians no longer serve shifts on the reference desk, and the Liaison Services Department handed off responsibility for some campus engagement activities (e.g., the library's participation in new student orientation) to a library standing committee.

Liaisons are available via appointment, email, and sometimes chat. They no longer staff a service point.

Liaisons do not staff the service/reference desk. They are available for research assistance through chat, email, phone, or in-person (appointment or walk-in).

Librarians no longer staff a reference desk. Implementation of more automated collection development processes.

Moves in the direction of less hands-on, more automated collection development. Many liaisons are taking on roles involving data management and open access.

No longer serving on the desk, focusing on consultations and embedding within departments. Reduced collection development spending and time spent on buying materials. Focus on filling faculty requests and supporting departmental needs more closely.

No reference desk staffing for academic department liaisons; far less focus on budget and resource management, collections infrastructure, shared instruction. For Learning Commons librarians, this has led to increase in areas served.

None of the above would be a better answer. Our liaisons have not shifted responsibilities but we are planning a major re-examination of our program, so this may come to pass.

Over the past year, liaison roles related to acquisitions have changed. The most significant change was a shifting away from liaison librarians selecting individual monographs, to a PDA-preferred approval plan without slips. This was in part done to redirect staff time to other priorities, such as new liaison roles.

Plan is for less time to be devoted to collection development and more time devoted to digital scholarship.

Recently, we began hiring more functional positions: data librarians, scholarly communications librarian, etc.

Reduced hours at the reference desk

Restructured Collection Management's monograph approval plan and shifted more towards demand-driven acquisition to create more aligned collections and to enable capacity of liaisons to integrate new roles. In reference and branch libraries, increased service desk staffing by non-librarians to create more availability of liaisons for consultations.

Review of approval books

SCAS technical services shifted to centralized processes. The organization has hired a collections strategist to help change overarching principles and daily practice.

Shifting away from reference desk duties and one-shot instruction, reduction in collection management tasks. This allows liaisons to have a greater role in upper-level instruction and consulting, where subject expertise is essential.

Shifting to two-tier reference so liaisons can concentrate on more in-depth consultation.

Since fall 2014, the libraries no longer have reference desks, and liaisons are not required to serve on the information desk, which replaced reference. We are trying to streamline a lot of liaison duties whenever possible by using technology and staff assistance.

Some liaisons no longer have regular reference desk duty.

Spending less time on reference desk

The addition of new areas of specialization, possibly paired liaisons for interdisciplinary work

The only shifting is fewer or no reference hours at the desks.

The subject experts will not be required to provide on-desk reference services. We are discussing how we support digital scholarship.

There has been more automation of collection development. In 1999, the HSL implemented a single service point and, gradually since then, librarians have focused their time on virtual service provision and outreach—a shift from in-library-based physical service provision. Liaisons have also used online instruction, LibGuides, and other means of meeting needs of larger groups. We have also expanded support staff roles to handle basic reference, and support of bibliographic software and other basic services, that also enables librarians to spend more of their time on services and roles that emerge.

They are no longer managing public service points. All public services/access services have been coordinated under one department.

This is a continuously evolving situation. Currently, as the Libraries has begun to place more focus on scholarly communication and its institutional repository this has become an added responsibility in conjunction with colleagues from a newly formed office of scholarly communications. Over the last decade, emphasis on collection development has diminished with the emergence of better approval plans and patron driven acquisition while focus on collection assessment has increased.

Those liaisons who had heavy reference responsibilities have been shifting the work to GAs and appointment-based rather than walk-up services.

We are likely to move away from enforced disciplinarity into a more flexible team-based approach in order to improve outreach and service on new priorities and shift our areas of engagement.

We are moving towards a single service desk with more efficient staffing for reference as a way to focus liaisons' work in new areas. We are currently assessing other ways to shift responsibilities.

We have had some shifting of responsibilities and anticipate more, pending increases in funding/staffing. Some collection management duties have been redistributed in order to allow the user engagement librarian to focus more on outreach. Some have increased their work on general instruction in order to free others for more in-depth subject liaison work. With more people, we could specialize more.

We play this by ear: each unit has different needs.

Yes, we closed our reference desk. We also assessed which workshops were actually needed and dropped others. But the greatest factor in being able to add "functional" liaisons was getting additional positions, not relinquishing tasks.

LIAISON TRAINING

31. **Do new liaisons receive training related to their new responsibilities?** N=66

Yes	60	91%
No	6	9%

If yes, please briefly describe the training that new liaisons receive. N=51

All liaisons receive basic training in data management and use of the library's high-tech spaces, including for large-scale visualization. They take the lead in working with researchers in their liaison departments and learn by doing. Peer-led seminars and workshops; external courses, seminars, workshops; custom introductory training on emerging research support areas including content mining, research data management, data visualization, and data analysis. Liaisons develop deeper subject matter expertise by attending seminars within departments and actively participating in discussions of disciplinary topics and research with faculty and students.

All liaisons receive training on The Open Access Harvester tool. There are regular trainings on newly acquired resources.

All librarians get mentoring; new librarians also receive training.

An orientation schedule was established for new employees to help them acclimate and help them learn about the organization.

As programs develop around data management support and scholarly communication, liaisons will be receiving training.

Collections training, instruction training, reference training

Could be orientation as a new employee, going to a workshop, going to a conference, etc.

Cross-training, team-teaching, coaching, internal and external workshops

Data management/curation, scholarly communications issues

Formal training program to support all of their activities throughout the year coupled with online materials.

Frequently, in the past it has been peer mentoring, a colleague who works in the same library. We are developing more structured and system-wide training modules.

Guidance from formal mentor, reporting officer; LibGuides and kickoff events

I'm not sure which new responsibilities this question refers to. If you are asking if new liaisons receive training, the answer is yes. Liaisons are oriented to their specific liaison role by their immediate supervisor. They are provided reports the prior liaison created, e.g., environmental scans, if this is not a new relationship. They are introduced to a key contact person within the constituent group they will be working with, who they may have already met during the recruitment process.

Informal at this point, as there has only been one recent new liaison.

Informed supervisors/orientation process

It depends on the library unit and the discipline.

Liaisons are provided with significant training in new areas. For example, our Data Library Coordinator, along with our Research Data Management Team, have provided—and continue to provide—training to support liaisons taking on the new roles of educating faculty about our data services support. Our Staff Development and Training Coordinator organizes Spring and Fall training events, as well as brown bag sessions, for all staff on a wide range of areas, include new areas of responsibilities for liaisons. The Libraries also provide access to a wide range of webinars relevant to new areas of responsibilities. In additions, librarians are well supported in their participation in training and development opportunities through the Libraries Staff Development and Training fund and their individual Professional Expense Reimbursement Fund.

Librarians new to the department receive a mentor within the department during the first year to assist them in learning their responsibilities. They meet with various individuals throughout the library to learn the processes they will need to perform their responsibilities. Meetings with the head of the department are scheduled for the first six months and may be scheduled on a regular basis or on an informal basis according to the needs of the individual liaison.

Meet with director of public services, director of collection management/scholarly communication; meet with functional specialists (open education resources, GIS, data management)

Mentoring tailored to the discipline and collection development training and public services orientation

Mentoring, etc.

Needs based: training on tools used, mentoring by more senior librarians, show & tell

New liaisons go through a rigorous training program in their department.

Newly hired liaisons meet with domain/functional experts to learn about scholarly communication, open access/agenda issues, etc.

Not as formal as it used to be, but it happens with new hires.

Not yet, but we will receive training on the IR. We've also received some small amount on copyright.

Orientation for new liaisons; training on subjects such as, book ordering, creating and maintaining LibGuides, and new technologies; group viewing of webinars; and monthly meetings on various topics of need.

Orientations to library organization, introductions to academic departments, training for use of library-specific tools, e.g., LibAnalytics and LibGuides, and instruction training.

Robust orientation plan includes training in instruction and collection development, work with an assigned mentor (an experienced liaison librarian), and meetings with departmental colleagues and heads of other library departments.

Senior liaisons provide mentoring. Acquisitions staff provide an orientation. New and old topics related to the liaison role are presented at twice monthly meetings.

Series of training and orientation sessions within the libraries system

The Engaged Librarian Forum provides professional development & context. The Teaching & Learning department and other functional specialists provide development opportunities.

The liaison coordinator offers approximately four sessions per year related to new and emerging areas of engagement (e.g., copyright, open access, research data management, ORCID, grant support). There is a concurrent expectation that liaisons will also engage in their own self-directed PD through participation in conferences, courses, personal reading and learning.

There is a liaison training checklist that covers all core job responsibilities, as well as basic library policy and procedures and university mission.

They are asked to read the papers that our liaisons have published to get an understanding of the program, the activities we pursue with and for our clients, and how the program has evolved over time. They shadow liaisons, take appropriate subject-based and other continuing education courses through the Medical Library Association and other venues, and we discuss at weekly departmental meetings.

This includes both formal and informal meetings with the faculty's supervisors and colleagues, as well as an ongoing education through meeting with academic department contacts.

This is an area of growth. Some librarians have attended workshops and conference programs to get more training. We have had cross training in some areas related to data management and scholarly communication. We are currently identifying needs and developing a longer-term plan for more targeted training in new areas to support digital scholarship.

Training comes from supervisors (coordinators), assigned mentors, peers via shadowing or informal advice, special training (for example from our Information Literacy unit, for best practices in BI), and access to webinars or in-house training opportunities.

Training for academic liaisons is primarily handled by their supervisors/coordinators.

Training has been somewhat ad hoc, largely through individual mentoring. We had no new liaisons for almost a decade, so are only now developing more formal training as we hire new librarians.

Training includes collections, instruction, reference desk, statistics keeping, etc.

Training varies across the divisions. The science division has created a training program focused on software packages that support the research lifecycle, as well as professional development workshops on things like presentation skills. The humanities division created a three-year training program called the Developing Librarian project focused on "re-skilling" the humanities librarians for digital humanities work. Other divisions benefit from a part-time training coordinator who arranges workshops, such as project management, and webinars on new skills and approaches.

We are currently launching a series of discussions and training sessions for all liaisons.

We developed a liaison checklist in 2013 that is completed in consultation with supervisors and colleagues. We promote webinars, conference attendances, peer training, etc.

We have a well-developed training program that is customized for each new librarian.

We have developed training manuals for both collections and outreach work. The collections manual was updated in the last c. 24 months, but the outreach manual is outdated. This latter will be updated as part of our re-examination of the liaison program. Training is received in collection and fund management. Disciplinary coordinators and department heads work with new liaisons to coach on methods for outreach, as well as fund management and materials selection. Training varies according to discipline served. We hold sessions called Reference Round Tables to coach liaisons/ reference staff, and our Instruction Unit holds sessions for those liaisons who do instruction.

We provide in-person or online training for in-house knowledge areas such as data management, scholarly communication, plagiarism, etc. We subscribe to webinars in areas of interest or training needs. We provide training funds for outside training on new areas of responsibility. We provide funding for travel to discipline-related conferences (in addition to library professional conferences)

We use our department meetings to discuss changes in scholarly communication. We also revamped our LibGuides content as part of our migration to LibGuides 2.0; librarians received training on both the technological side of the upgrade, as well as the pedagogy underlying the use of LibGuides.

Workshops on scholarly communication activities, new acquisition system, etc.

Yes, in the form of an online toolkit and some training at the departmental level. There has been minimal training involving the use of our online ordering system, setting up profiles, and accounting issues. Plans are in place to improve training.

32. Please indicate the professional development and continuing education opportunities that are available to liaisons at your library. Check all that apply. N=64

Dedicated funding and support for conference attendance	62	97%
Internal cross-training and professional development	60	94%
Dedicated funding and support for external workshops and continuing education programs	59	92%
Dedicated funding and support for participation in formal classes and degree programs	45	70%
Other opportunity	14	22%

Please briefly describe the other opportunity. N=14

All librarians can participate in up to 10 research days per year, study leaves, and research leaves, in accordance with policies and agreements for all librarians.

All of those are available to all librarians, so are not specific to liaisons.

All librarians receive an allotment for professional development to be used to participate in continuing education opportunities.

Can request and often get funding for workshops, continuing education programs, and classes.

Funding provided on a case-by-case basis for external workshops and continuing education programs.

Liaisons can apply for funding from our Staff Development and Training fund to support participation in external workshops, CE programs, and conference attendance. They aren't allocated a specific amount, but there is dedicated funding for this annually.

Library subscription to lynda.com

Mentoring by colleagues

Newly developed library instruction training program headed the Learning and Outreach Teams, which is a professional development program designed to create a culture of teaching excellence at the libraries and based on ACRL standards for proficiency for instruction librarians.

On occasion, we do support additional training as needed.

Professional development funding is available to all librarians, not just liaisons, so there isn't dedicated funding specifically for liaison responsibilities. At HSL, we encourage liaisons to attend discipline specific conferences and sometimes these are funded by the school they serve. The university offers tuition waivers (one course per semester) and we make adjustments to allow interested liaisons to take advantage of that employee benefit.

Some course work and continuing education is supported.

The formal classes/degree programs are short-term, and usually a certificate, not a diploma.

We have a formal mentoring program.

33. **Please briefly describe opportunities liaisons have to meet as a group to discuss issues, projects, or techniques for effective liaison work.** N=55

2x/month departmental meetings

A few years ago we developed broad subject-based Teaching Communities.

A monthly meeting of the Library Liaison Group, as well as a monthly meeting of the Library Collections Forum

All liaisons are invited to monthly research writing group. All liaisons have monthly meetings to discuss instruction, scholarly communications, collections, research services, outreach.

All subject librarian liaisons meet four times a year as a group. Each of the five subject coordinators holds regular meetings. Special programs take place as needed.

Brown Bags, Research Coffee, IL symposium

Department meetings and Collection Team meetings (by broad disciplinary cohort, e.g., Social Sciences, Sciences, Global Studies, Arts and Humanities, etc.), and a monthly Collections Forum for subject liaisons

Department meetings, brown bag lunches, First Thursdays (a once-a-month program that highlights specific projects for all of the library)

Department meetings, teaching roundtable, "affinity" group, discipline/subject groups

Departmental meetings and retreats

Departmental meetings, "Keeping Up" workshops, informal meetings

Departmental meetings, brown bags, librarian forum (internal), discipline-based affinity groups

Director of public services, director of collection management/scholarly communication meet regularly with liaisons as a group to discuss issues and work on projects.

Engaged Librarian Forum, webinars

Have committees and listservs.

In addition to the monthly meetings, there is a subject librarian steering group, and a Research and Development Digital Scholarship Think Tank to discuss new technologies, digital scholarship working groups, and occasional brown bag lunch meetings.

In the past, liaisons have met at least quarterly to discuss issues, projects, journal articles, and other techniques. These can be formal or informal meetings. Depending on the topic, guest presenters can be invited.

ISR department meetings every two weeks, special topic-focused meetings and training opportunities, annual retreats for training and teaching

Journal clubs, informal meetings among themselves, team building events such as pizza parties and picnics just for liaisons, etc.

Liaison Team meetings are scheduled throughout the academic year.

Liaisons have the opportunity to discuss their work during divisional meetings and within library-wide strategic development groups.

Liaisons meet as a department once a week. Additional meetings/discussions are scheduled as needed.

Liaisons meet every other month as a group, in what is called the Subject Specialists meeting. Additionally, each disciplinary group meets every other month, approximately.

Liaisons meet informally to share information and discuss projects, new technology, etc. At HSL, as mentioned earlier, liaisons from across the library have two group meetings a month (on different days and times to accommodate varying schedules). These are opportunities to seek advice and share tips and projects, etc. One of the liaison librarians convenes these meetings and calls for and contributes agenda items.

Liaisons meet together twice monthly to discuss issues and provide feedback on instruction and collection development matters.

Many of our liaisons are organized into broad disciplinary sections (Social Sciences, Science/Engineering, Humanities). These groups meet frequently. We also have collection development discussion groups, meetings to discuss scholarly communication issues, etc. Disciplinary sections have retreats they use to reflect on their work.

Meetings of our councils, as described earlier, of our subject teams, within buildings, a series of brown bag lunches, meetings of the Liaison Assembly

Monthly departmental meetings, series of outreach & engagement workshops, planned informal discussions and online forum

Monthly meetings at each campus site, annual liaison summit across sites

Monthly meetings of all liaisons, email discussions

Monthly meetings plus "Communities of Interest" to discuss themes relevant to the four areas of the Libraries Engagement Framework

Monthly meetings

Monthly staff meeting with all subject librarians and reference desk staff. Periodic collection management meetings with subject librarians. Monthly subject team meetings. Some community of practice sponsored events.

Monthly subject department and Collection Development Council meetings

Project teams meet regularly as needed. The Research Librarians meet as a group. Lightning talks are scheduled to share projects in progress across the libraries.

Regular departmental meetings, continuing education forums

Regularly schedule meetings that bring liaisons together, related to the training

Regularly scheduled forums for liaisons to discuss issues and share practices

Subject specialists meet monthly.

Team meetings, area meetings, all liaison meetings, work groups

The Director for Liaison and Instruction Services has been offering lunch-time forums on designated topics and tools available for liaisons. We have identified and are initiating cross-disciplinary sub-groups to provide informal collaborative discussions and possible projects.

The Health Science Center library liaisons have meetings scheduled weekly (although probably 25% of them are canceled due to scheduling conflicts) and liaison activities can be placed on the agenda. All liaisons live in the same suite, so there is ample opportunity to discuss new initiatives, what has worked, what hasn't.

The liaisons meet regularly in their broad subject groups (Social Sciences, Humanities, Life Sciences, etc.) All liaisons also attend a monthly meeting for information and training.

The Liaison Services Department has a standing weekly meeting, an annual full-day retreat, and many opportunities for informal interaction because all our offices are in a shared suite.

The Libraries holds regularly scheduled subject librarian meetings, as well as smaller meetings for discipline groups.

The recent ARL sponsored liaison institute at Cornell has provided us a platform to have discussion about liaison work. Previous to that gathering, we had committees and task forces dedicated to various aspects of liaison work, such as a research data management committee that discussed training and service provision.

There are many opportunities for liaisons to meet. Again, brown bags, spring and fall training opportunities, as well as meetings within their units, and specific project meetings/events are all venues for discussion.

Various department meetings, informal networking, interest group sessions, brown bag meetings

Various work groups and task forces including research, instruction, and outreach; standing committee on professional advancement, etc.

We have a liaison planning committee that organizes training and programming.

We have bimonthly meetings of all subject librarians to share knowledge, strategies, etc. We have an email discussion list. We have an online toolbox of templates, contact information, news, and content for knowledge areas such as scholarly communications and open access. In the near future, we plan to assign coordinators to facilitate communications within subject-related groups (share best practices, identify training needs, etc.)

We have monthly "all selectors" meetings, monthly meetings of the Research and Information Services division, ad hoc meetings to discuss specific projects. Our offices are concentrated in one area, which leads to much informal discussion. Also much email discussion.

We have recently piloted cross-departmental and cross-functional teams that either include liaison librarians or tackle aspects of liaison. We are using these pilots to encourage greater collaboration among staff. Liaison librarians, along with others, are free to set up and collaborate in working groups for short-duration projects, either organically or through existing system-wide committees (e.g., Reference, Instruction). One of our suburban campuses has regular weekly meetings of all its liaison librarians.

We hold weekly meetings in addition to training meetings, which occur 1x month.

Weekly meeting of all reference and clinical services personnel

ADMINISTRATION OF LIAISON SERVICES

34. Please select the one choice below that best describes how liaison services are coordinated and facilitated in your library. N=66

Self-administered by each liaison	27	41%
Centrally administered by a liaison coordinator or manager	9	14%
Centrally administered by a liaison committee	6	9%
Centrally administered by library administration	4	6%
Other administrative structure	20	30%

Please briefly describe the other administrative structure. N=20

A small team of research librarian coordinators coordinates much of the liaison program.

Academic liaisons work across administrative lines. For example, the Director of Collections works directly with academic liaisons but most do not report directly to that position. They also work directly with the Coordinator of Information Literacy.

Administered by departmental manager, but collaboratively.

Broadly focused department heads such as Area Studies, Sciences, Social Sciences, and Arts & Humanities

Combination of a liaison manager and the Associate Dean

Combination of the above

Coordinated at department or library level

Coordinated at the level of the unit libraries

Coordinated through the Associate Dean of User Services and the Associate Dean and Director for the Medical Sciences Library, and to some extent the Libraries' other associate deans.

Coordinator + team approach + self-directed, a little of each above

Coordinator leads steering group for subject librarians.

Generally self administered, but each liaison reports up through a department chair who stays abreast of their activities.

Highly collaborative single department jointly managed by two department heads with defined functional responsibilities (instruction/outreach and collections/research support).

Liaison assignments (who liaises to what group) is administered by department head, but the individual activities are self-administered by each liaison, as each department, college, or academic program has unique information needs.

Liaison work is coordinated via the Libraries' Unit Heads Committee, comprised of branch heads, public services AULs, and UL.

Right now it's centrally administered by library administration but we're moving towards the liaison and their direct supervisor having more control over the process.

Services are coordinated by library directors for each of our four universities, as described earlier, and by the User Services Council and the Library Resources Council.

The liaison coordinator manages communications among the large group of liaisons, suggests training opportunities, and trains new liaisons. Because liaisons report to many different departments within the library and serve departments with vastly different needs, liaisons do a lot of self-administration as well. At HSL, because most of the liaisons are organizationally located in the User Services Department, the department managers group, who meet weekly, typically is the place where decisions regarding liaison services are discussed, decided, or recommended to the liaison group or to library administration, as needed. If liaisons in other departments will be affected, they and their supervisors are brought into the discussion.

We have functioned fairly independently but are introducing more coordination.

While each liaison does self-administer, we have a leadership team for liaison services. This team leads strategic planning for the Academic Liaison Program and develops, provides, or facilitates training for liaisons.

35. To whom do liaisons report? Check all that apply. N=67

To their respective department heads	40	60%
Different reporting lines for different liaisons	29	43%
Associate Dean for Public Services/Collection Development	20	30%
Head of Reference	16	24%
Head of appropriate subject division	16	24%
Single reporting line	12	18%
Collection Development officer	8	12%
Associate Dean for Technical Services	4	6%
Head of Cataloging	3	5%
Head of Acquisitions	2	3%
Other reporting line	15	22%

Please briefly describe the other reporting line. N=15

Assistant Director for Academic Liaison, Associate Director for Collections and Academic Services, GIS and Data Department Head, Head, DC Regional Libraries

Associate Dean of Academic Affairs

Branch library directors and associate deans

Depending on the responsibility, a liaison would report to the AD for Collections for collection development, the Director for Liaison and Instruction for most liaison roles, the Head of Reference for research consultation and reference services (that is currently under transition and redefinition). All liaisons are still evaluated by their library director as their primary supervisor.

Head of Collection Development (We have more than one collection development librarian.)

Head, Learner Support and Engagement Services

Jointly report to two department heads (functions as a single reporting line).

Many report to the Director of the Academic Liaison Program (ALP). The director and those who report to her comprise the ALP Leadership Team.

Most liaisons who are subject experts report to a manager who reports to the AUL for Research. Others report to managers who report to the AUL of Learning & Teaching, AUL for Publishing, and AUL for Health Sciences.

Team Leader for Research Services, which includes collections, reference and instruction

They all end up reporting to the Associate University Librarian.

Those operating in branch libraries report to collection management/scholarly communication and director of special collections/branch libraries.

To library directors in our Camden, New Brunswick, and Health Sciences locations and to the associate university librarian for research and instructional services in our New Brunswick location.

To their specific department head, which then report to their library director, who then reports to the AUL for Research and Learning Services.

Two lines, science and humanities supervisors who are also liaisons and then to AD.

36. Who is responsible for evaluating liaisons' performance? N=67

Liaisons report to various supervisors who are also responsible for evaluation of liaison	32	48%
Liaisons report to various supervisors, while other library leaders provide input to evaluation	19	28%
Liaisons all report to the same supervisor	8	12%
Liaisons all report to the same set of supervisors	3	5%
Liaison performance is not evaluated	1	2%
Other evaluation method	4	6%

Please briefly describe the other evaluation method. N=4

Evaluation is part of our faculty processes and includes annual reviews for the untenured and five-year reviews for the tenured, as well as the reappointment and tenure reviews.

In addition to supervisor, there is peer evaluation through librarian contractual process.

Liaisons are evaluated by their primary supervisor, typically the campus library director. Input on evaluation is provided by AD for Collections, Director for Liaison and Instruction Services, Head of Research and Reference Services; also the chair of any university library committee on which they serve.

The two heads of Liaison Services jointly evaluate liaisons' performance.

37. What criteria are used to evaluate liaison responsibilities? N=66

Evaluation criteria include liaison functions	33	50%
Goal-based evaluation	20	30%
Evaluation criteria do not specifically cover liaison functions	3	5%
Liaisons are not evaluated	0	0%
Other criteria	10	15%

Please briefly describe the other criteria. N=10

All librarians submit a faculty statement of activities. Annual reviews are based on professional performance (including student teaching evaluations where applicable), service, and creative activity/scholarship.

Both liaison functions and goal-based

Evaluation includes evaluation criteria and goal-based evaluations.

Evaluations are very open-ended. Some specifically cover liaison functions and some do not. HSL uses goal-based evaluations.

Liaisons set specific goals and objectives and the appraisal process addresses them.

Our evaluation criteria include liaison functions, as well as goal-based evaluation.

Peer review process

Quantitative data is collected on instruction and research consultations. There is an annual self-assessment that is a part of individual liaisons' yearly evaluations. We are working on collecting more detailed information on liaison activities.

This depends on whether the liaison role is primary or secondary. For primary, the answer is liaison functions. For secondary, liaison evaluations have input from disciplinary coordinators. Each librarian sets their goals in conversation with their supervisor, and these goals include liaison work.

We use both goal-based evaluation and evaluation criteria that include liaison functions.

EVALUATION OF LIAISON SERVICES

38. Does your library compile statistics documenting liaison activities? N=67

Yes	63	94%
No	4	6%

If yes, what statistics are collected? N=56

All contacts, whether at the individual, class, or departmental level, are recorded.

Although we do not track liaison work directly, we compile statistics for many of the areas that they work in, e.g., reference, instruction, collection development.

Classes, research appointments

Consultations, instruction, reference (virtual and F2F)

Consultations, outreach activities (including one-on-one meetings and large orientations), and events. Instruction and reference statistics are also collected by our Learning Services and Reference Services Programs, respectively.

Consultations, teaching, outreach/programming

Contacts (both reference contacts and consultations), instruction sessions

Examples include number of user contacts, length of contacts, level of contacts, number of searches, number of documents delivered, etc.

Faculty interactions, research interviews, instruction sessions

Has not been strong before, working on it.

In-person and virtual consultations/reference statistics, engagement on research projects, office hours, collaborative relationships with departments/programs/offices/faculty, instruction sessions

Instruction

Instruction and off-desk consultation

Instruction and reference numbers

Instruction sessions, research consultations

Instruction sessions, research consultations, email and chat reference transactions, circulation statistics by call number, interlibrary loan statistics by call number

Instruction sessions, physical and virtual reference questions and consultations

Instruction, consultations

Instruction, consultations, reference questions, mediated searches

Instruction, consultations, some collection development (materials endowment spending)

Instruction, reference transactions, consultations

Instruction, reference, consultations

Instruction, reference

Instruction, consultations, outreach, reference

Instruction, consultation

Instructional activities, consultations, collections spending

Liaisons record their interactions in our RefAnalytics database and apply the READ scale. This gives us a sense of the level of complexity of the questions.

Liaisons track instruction sessions, consultations, major projects, grant funding received, user comments, publications and presentations, inquiries and proactive activities, and sometimes other data that their constituent group's administration may be interested in.

Library instructions statistics, including number of participants and time spent; reference transactions, including number and type of transaction, as well as time spent; office consultations, including number and time spent; faculty support statistics.

Number of instruction sessions, number of students reached, reference consultations

Number of interactions, with whom, and using what communication process (in person, email, phone, etc.)

Number of one-shot classes taught and tours given

Number of research consultations and instruction sessions

Number of research consultations, number of research sessions taught, and number of reference transactions. We would like to measure impacts of liaison work and are now just beginning to determine those metrics.

Number of sessions conducted, and head count for students seen; tracking of one-on-one reference and advice contacts

Number of sessions, participants

On-going conversation about what to collect

Quantitative statistics such as the number of consultations, instructional sessions, reference questions, and student feedback from instruction sessions

Reference and instruction

Reference consultations, classes taught, tours offered

Reference, instruction, consultation statistics (both quantitative and qualitative), events hosted/consulted on in library's visualization and technology spaces

Reference questions, consults, instruction

Reference questions/consultations, instructional sessions

Reference transactions, teaching, research consultations

Research consultations, instruction

Research consultations, reference questions, instruction sessions taught, etc.

Statistics for faculty/student collection requests; research consultations provided by subject; reference desk statistics; instruction sessions by department, session type, and class size; number of research/course guides created; number of tours and orientations; number of outreach opportunities provided by department

Stats in RefTracker and Digital Measures

Teaching, consultation, and reference encounters are all documented.

We collect ARL statistics related to liaison activity, including the number of instruction sessions offered and the number of unique individuals attending the instruction sessions.

We collect data on various types of consultative and instructional activities, including: time spent in prep and in direct engagement, the modality of engagement, the type of service that is engaged, and the demographic information of the department and individuals served.

We collect instruction statistics.

We gather statistics on instruction and research consultation sessions, as well as tracking collection expenditures for those liaisons who have collection portfolios.

We keep statistics on instruction, research consultations, and office hours in academic departments.

We use a home-grown system to collect input stats (knowledge transactions in a liaison role (could be reference, instruction, consultation, presentations at departments), or other activities like attending seminars, department meetings, etc.

Yes, though these statistics may or may not be shared, interpreted, and used for continual improvement.

Additional Comments N=2

Not currently, we are trying to define new structures and categories for which we should collect statistics. ARL stats are still collected for reference and instruction, but those are seen as increasingly incomplete as reflections of liaison activities.

Not yet

39. Has there been any formal evaluation of the effectiveness of liaison services? N=66

Yes	32	49%
No	34	51%

If yes, please indicate the method of evaluation. Check all that apply. N=32

Tracked number of instruction sessions	32	100%
Tracked number of reference/research interviews	31	97%

Conducted user surveys	20	63%
Interviewed members of department(s)	12	38%
Tracked number of department meetings attended by liaisons	9	28%
Conducted focus groups	9	28%
Other evaluation method	9	28%

Please briefly describe the other evaluation method. N=9

April 2015 external review: reviewers held confidential meetings with over 50 senior leaders and administrators across the university about how the library engages with faculty.

Data from accreditation studies, data from 3rd party survey instruments, coordination with grant rates/patient care outcomes/student success

Department meetings attended is an optional statistic.

Developed a matrix and used self-reported scoring to measure liaison engagement with departments.

How well is the liaison integrated into their assigned units—committees, teams, workgroups, projects. Note that the willingness of the unit to work with the liaison is also considered (no matter how good the liaison, some units just refuse to play).

More is not necessarily better, quality of interactions and strategic impact are valued greatly.

On a couple occasions, a library school student has done a paper or report for the library. In one example, a student interviewed each of the liaisons and conducted a focus group session and provided a detailed report in which the information was de-identified. This provided data on how much time liaisons estimated they spent on those activities, how much time spent learning domain subject knowledge, the types of services they felt their groups most valued, and similar information.

Review of evaluations from instruction sessions and/or workshops

Would like to use new methods soon.

Additional Comments N=2

Although we trace the number of instruction sessions, reference interviews, department meetings, I'd say that we have not used these for formal evaluation of liaison services. We have not articulated desired outcomes or evaluated the effectiveness of our services. We have conducted LibQUAL+®, but it has been some time ago.

We don't look at any of these measures on a systematic basis, but do occasionally observe some of these trends in our data.

40. Please identify indicators of success for your library's liaison program. Check all that apply. N=61

New partnerships across campus	58	95%
Increased number of consultations	52	85%
Increased number of classes	49	80%
Recognition from library and other professional organizations	24	39%

Retention of liaisons	20	33%
Additional funding from the university	19	31%
Other indicator	19	31%

Please briefly describwe the other indicator. N=19

Although not formalized, we attempt to stay aware of new or increased social capital that the library acquires through faculty engagement activities, for example, how often we are invited to participate in pan-campus projects, grants, initiatives, problem-solving.

Anecdotally, we get unsolicited feedback and "thank you" emails and comments on LibQUAL+® and other surveys that specifically mention a subject librarian.

Comments and feedback from faculty and students.

Comments from faculty members who have seen value as a result of liaison work.

Current area of exploration.

Data and comments from regularly conducted LibQUAL+® surveys that indicate effective liaison services provided by the Libraries and specific librarians.

Do you mean things that would indicate success if they happened or things that we have actually experienced? At HSL, recognition by deans and other administrators of the value of liaisons to faculty and students (in public statements and in meetings); financial support from some of the schools and hospital units served; adjunct faculty appointments and promotions in the schools; testimonials from users; incorporation in grants and in large team projects (systematic reviews, accreditation teams); committee appointments and invitations to specific events; access to faculty listservs; co-authorships and acknowledgments.

Feedback from faculty/researchers regarding value of liaisons. Recent Ithaka survey results certainly spoke to the values of subject librarians in particular.

Feedback from students and faculty, repeat visits/requests

High satisfaction ratings from faculty/students for liaison services reported via annual library survey.

Liaisons' personal assessment of their ability to provide services to their assigned area(s).

Recognition by those we serve, identification of the librarians as significant contributors to the university's mission

Recognition from faculty and students (e.g., thank you letters, and letters of reference for librarians' academic reviews)

Recognition from the department or colleges

Recognition from university and faculty

That instructors ask liaisons to teach year after year; unsolicited emails of endorsement; academic faculty willing to collaborate with library faculty on major projects; joint appointments in academic departments or centers/institutes; academic units funding librarian travel to conference; requests from academic units for library to develop and teach unique subject- or information-based courses; academic faculty asking library faculty to serve on their grants.

The rate of adoption of new forms of services (researcher profiling, e.g., data management)

Trying to develop definition of success—working on this.

We are planning on utilizing both quantitative feedback such as number of sessions taught, as well as liaison's own impressions of how goals are going and informal feedback from departments (do they know who their liaison is, etc.)

41. What methods of communication have been established to ensure that information gathered by liaisons is considered in the library's decision-making processes? N=53

Administrators attend monthly liaison meetings.

Analysis and feedback from data collection, debriefings with liaisons

Both personal communication with department leadership and with Associate Dean

Department meetings with UL/AUL and liaisons, feedback through various channels

Department meetings, retreats, library newsletters

Detailed statistics, strategic planning conversations, sharing information with appropriate Associate Director

Email, meetings

Email

Faculty meetings, annual reviews through supervisors

Feedback from departments on collection needs is reported via a content advisory group made up of subject librarians. Monthly liaison meetings are one way that liaisons communicate with associate deans who may attend. Liaison coordinator meets with Associate Dean of Collection Development and Access and the Associate Dean for Research & Learning Services and to the Dean of Libraries.

Feedback from students and faculty, repeat visits/requests

Frequent meetings of liaisons and subject teams and with supervisors, department heads, and associate directors to discuss faculty and student needs and service strategies. Annual Activity Reports are reviewed and discussed in the appraisal process, so that emerging challenges, solutions, trends, and accomplishments can be shared among administrators and taken into consideration during decision making. A structured Library Representatives group brings together faculty and graduate students from all academic departments with the vice provost & director of libraries, other administrators, and the liaisons, to share information and discuss library resources, services, and strategies.

Information is located on an intranet and may be accessed by any library staff or faculty member.

Information is solicited from liaisons by the department heads, who communicate it to their associate dean in regular (biweekly) meetings. Liaisons may also contribute to targeting information-gathering efforts related to the library budget or strategic directions.

Information literacy assessments, strategic planning metrics

Liaisons are members of most library committees. Liaisons communicate issues directly to their department chairs and AUL for Public Services as well as the AUL over collection development. Liaisons meet formally as a group in the Library Liaison Group and the group's chair meets monthly with the AUL for Public Services.

Liaisons bring info to "reference" department meeting and it is funneled by department head to HSCL director. Liaisons bring info to HSCL senior management meeting, which the director attends. Liaisons email director directly (copying reference head).

Liaisons communicate frequently with their disciplinary sections and department heads. There are also cross-library groups that communicate around: collections coordination, public services, department heads.

Liaisons make their information known to their representatives on one of our councils, their cabinet member, or the faculty planning and coordinating committee—or all of the above! Development of our current strategic plan included broad participation from across the library system, including liaisons.

Liaisons participate in strategic planning activities.

Liaisons participated in the creation of the new library strategic plan.

Liaisons report comments in the Faculty Interaction Database. Liaisons are expected to report out important news to their departments. Liaisons also write annual summaries, and quarterly reports are generated at the departmental level.

Liaisons report to divisional directors who sit on a management committee. The directors report to the management committee or the AUL for collections and services on feedback from liaisons about faculty and student needs.

Liaisons' feedback is always considered when making decisions.

Mainly communication at each department level, with direct supervisors who then share that information with members of the administration.

Monthly all-liaison meetings, statistics

Monthly meetings with departments and department heads focused on collection-related issues where collections issues are discussed, representative working group (Collections and Access Working Group) that discusses and makes decisions.

Monthly meetings, as indicated above, regular meetings of team leaders with the AD of Research and Information Services, appointment of liaisons to relevant committees

Monthly meetings, informal communication

NA, though we plan to review this as part of our review of liaison services.

No one formal method of communication

None that I know of.

Not much. AD is on management team. AD works with department. Would like to see more broad strategic planning.

Nothing formal established, but it would be nice. Liaison librarians do prepare impact statements for proposed additions to the curriculum, and that may influence decision-making for collection development.

Now: Through group meetings and managing up through supervisors to the program director and the AUL for Academic Services. Future: All of the above plus data gathered through a customer relationship management system.

On-going. Being explored by a team of librarians.

One-on-one meetings between liaisons and supervisors. Established a Liaison Council for all liaisons to share ideas and establish best practices. Department meetings open to all liaisons.

Participate in library review process ahead of strategic planning. Participate in annual departmental goal setting. Provide feedback on project charters, proposal, job descriptions. Invited to contribute to conversations on emerging issues via ISR meetings and special meetings. Participate in library-wide staff meetings.

Provide an annual report to library administration, liaise with the library's Office of Assessment, and hold monthly meetings to share.

Quarterly reports, Collection Managers Forum, and the Engaged Librarian Forum

Reporting up through supervisor, although this is not formal.

Small group meetings when decisions need to be made.

Statistical and anecdotal information is gathered and applied.

Still working on this.

Team meetings, area meetings, review of feedback by supervisors and administrators, collection development analysis, ILL analysis

There are various methods of communications in place to ensure information from liaisons feeds into decision making. Many liaisons sit on at least one or two committees/working groups and their insights inform direction of work within those groups. Information gleaned from liaisons is often brought to decision making discussions by unit heads in that context of that committee.

This is supposed to happen through Library Engagement Team meetings.

Unit meeting, reporting up the chain of command

Use of data from Wufoo, clinical studies as a component of our strategic planning, feedback from constituents

We actively solicit input from liaisons related to specific questions/issues. Also "bullet" points and other informal communications.

We have an online system to direct requests for books, DVDs, and other small one-time purchases to liaisons for approval before final decisions are made by collection development staff. Requests for resources with recurring costs or for major one-time purchases are gathered by liaisons and forwarded to the Collection Development team for final purchase decisions. The library's Strategic Planning Team has recently consulted with the Liaisons Team members when developing potential goals and initiatives.

We regularly report both the quantity and the type of interactions to the Five Year Indicators report that is submitted annually to the provost. The AD who supervises most of the liaisons is part of the executive group and the strategic planning group.

Yearly gathering of information by department heads/managers for library retreat with managers and the Libraries' administration. Yearly gathering of information by department heads/managers for strategic planning. Subject librarian meetings are held on a regular basis and notes are forwarded to the appropriate leaders for consideration. Annual self-evaluations are reviewed by a number of directs and associate deans.

BENEFITS AND CHALLENGES OF LIAISON SERVICES

42. Please describe up to three top benefits from providing liaison services. N=62

Ability to contribute to faculty research and student success at institution. Ability to serve as college-neutral space for bringing together disciplines to foster scholarly communication across campus. Ability to impact course and assignment design.

Ability to provide high-level research services and educational services. Ability to gather frontline information about current research and educational directions at the university. Integration into the university community.

Being out of the library and in the users' environment prompts questions and connections that would have been missed otherwise. Close relationships with individual users and groups of users; users have a go-to person (for anything) and recognizable contact with the library. Services are based on knowledge of the population served and customized accordingly.

Benefit for faculty, students, and staff to have a single point of contact with the library. Benefit to library and to liaisons that collection development, instruction, and reference inform each other. Benefit to university and academic departments because they have an advocate inside the library.

Better communication from departments to library. Better communication from library to departments. Higher library visibility across campus.

Better education for students, faculty and staff on information literacy. Better collections that reflect university needs. Targeted programs based on department or college.

Better service to faculty and students. Deeper engagement in the research, teaching, and learning process. Sense of professional identity.

Better understanding of the needs of programs and departments in order to respond appropriately to campus needs. Increased student and faculty use of the library. We are working towards a student body with stronger information literacy skills at graduation.

Builds strong relationship with departments, providing key contact who ensures their needs are met. Leverages librarian expertise in specific subject areas.

Close communication and collaboration with academic departments and other groups external to the libraries. Increased recognition of how librarians help achieve the university's mission. Increased ability to develop expertise and anticipate or respond to our users' needs.

Close connections to departments. Specialization—liaisons develop expertise in certain areas that is valuable. Provides a human face for library.

Close relationships with faculty, which help us develop better services. Positive feedback from departments is beneficial during our budgeting process. We can more easily identify campus-wide trends in their early stages.

Closer relationships with faculty and students. Higher visibility for the library and its services. Library is viewed as an active partner in the academic enterprise.

Connection to the faculty who drive the curriculum. Visibility for the Libraries. More seamless support for students if librarians are directly involved in subject area.

Demonstrate value to communicate. Personalize relationships with department. Increase collaboration opportunities.

Develop relationships with research faculty and contribute to the development of strong teaching and learning across the campus. Ability to engage and support learners. Increased profile of Libraries and Cultural Resources across campus and within the broader community.

Development of close relationships to academic units. Subject expertise makes support more effective. More informed acquisitions decisions and collection management.

Direct contact with departments, faculty, and students (2-way communication). Provides level of instructional expertise within library staff. Provides high-level collection development and curation knowledge because of working relationships with department.

Direct involvement with faculty and students in academic departments helps make planning more user-focused. Liaison work increases opportunities for instruction and increases awareness and use of our collections. Liaison work increases opportunities to be partners in ongoing scholarly endeavors.

Engages the Libraries in the research and educational life of the university. Allows us to understand user needs and act on them.

Enhancing the university's research capacity and competitiveness. Informing the Libraries' strategic planning, directions, and investments. Leveraging the knowledge of disciplinary librarians to facilitate resource discovery and promote services and capabilities of the library that contribute to faculty and student success.

Faculty and students receive customized, expert support services. The library's collections are better matched to user needs.

Faculty find the tailored support and expertise extremely valuable. Through the liaisons library administration can learn about the specific needs of departments and faculty. The libraries are integrated into departments in a diverse range of support that reflects the variety of disciplinary needs.

Formal engagement with campus community. Personal and professional satisfaction. Gaining knowledge about needs and desires of campus community.

Good communication with faculty/students. Faculty/student satisfaction with liaison and library services. One point person for all library info and questions.

Greater awareness of teaching and research trends. Opportunities to promote library services and resources, including information literacy. Immerse library into faculty and student work stream.

Greater visibility and relevance to university community and research life cycle. Ability to partner on research activities in academic and non-academic departments. Greater understanding of value of librarian work by external stakeholders.

Improve outcomes for researchers and students. Tailor the library collection to campus needs. Stay aware of new scholarly trends and needs.

Improved relationships with and closer ties to everyone on campus. These relationships help with student retention and help us create a stronger library collection. Better visibility of issues important to libraries (information literacy, open access, etc.) and opportunities for influence on curriculum, campus priorities, etc. Better opportunities to develop point-of-need assistance through instruction, consultation, etc., where that assistance is most useful.

Improves communication with academic departments. Encourages support of the library and its mission. Guides our spending of collection development funds.

Increased communication. Support for student/faculty research and success.

Increased engagement with departmental research needs. Targeted support for graduate and undergraduate students. New partnerships.

Increased engagement with the library and the value added to research, teaching, and learning. Increased support for the library. Ensuring the ongoing relevance of the library to the university.

Increased familiarity with library service in the academic departments. Increased awareness of academic department needs in the libraries. Integration of the library in the academic life of the university.

Increased perceived value of libraries/librarians to faculty. Support for teaching and research efforts. Improved library understanding of departments' needs.

Increased student success. Increased research productivity. Increased national recognition.

Informed collections/content building. Better awareness of Libraries resources and information literacy/research skills. Improved research outcomes (higher quality papers/assignments, etc.)

Integral role in health sciences center, now key component of health sciences center planning. Participation in curriculum development and research design. Library has much higher profile with users, esp. faculty and administrators.

Integrates the library and its expertise into the professional curricula of the Health Sciences Center. Develops close professional relationships among liaisons and faculty/administrators from the Health Science Center, building collaborations to strategically plan, collaborate on projects and grants, understand and meet the priorities of the HSC. Proactively brings students into the library and provides them with the sense that it is their "home away from home".

Involvement with faculty and student research. Liaisons are included in developing teaching and learning strategies and objectives. Library is seen as a partner in institutional mission and programs.

Keeps the Libraries relevant. Establishing good relationships with patrons. Helps create effective collection strategies.

Knowledge of the changing needs of academic departments and programs. Spreading awareness of library services and support. Connections with liaison librarians at other institutions covering same subject areas.

Learning about the current priorities in schools and academic departments. The creation of partnerships with faculty that are intellectually stimulating and have impact on teaching, research, and learning on campus. Students are better researchers and ultimately better-informed citizens resulting from research sessions and consultations.

Librarians are essential partners in teaching and research, raising recognition of the library's value. Librarians have opportunities to increase knowledge in areas of interest to users (e.g., copyright, OA, data management). The library learns about user needs and preferences through liaisons' interactions with users.

Library is aware of what is happening within the department. Partnerships. Customization.

Making connections and building relationships with faculty in other departments. Opportunity to promote library services. Insight into collection and service needs of departments.

Meeting constituent needs. Improved partnerships. Increased visibility of the library.

More pro-active involvement with university departments and student interactions. Greater visibility for library across campus. Use of professional time for strategic goals.

Provide research assistance to faculty and students. Provide instruction to faculty and students to more effectively use library resources and services. Develop collections to support scholarship and research.

Provides a way to bring current resources and services directly to faculty and students. Brings information about research/teaching/data/resource needs within department back to the libraries. Gathers information we need to determine future direction of the library.

Provides one knowledgeable point of contact for faculty and students. Promotes library resources and services.

Provides subject expertise and research support to students and faculty. Assures that materials obtained by the library are relevant and useful to students and faculty. Enriches teaching and learning experiences of students and faculty through collaboration and use of library resources.

Researchers and students have one point person for all their library needs. Provide expertise that can help support the research lifecycle. Reduce the burden of researchers by saving them time.

Responsive and tailored library services and resource to our various communities of users across the disciplines. Improved funding to support library services, facilities, and staffing. Development of an informed information literacy program that mirrors priorities of the university's strategic initiatives.

Simplify a complex library system by providing single-person first point of contact. Better understanding of individual faculty needs, priorities, pain points. Opportunities to engage with faculty and departments to better understand how to structure library services.

Strengthens ties between the library and the community. Allows for currency of service provision and ensures we are providing excellent and relevant service. Integrates information literacy into the intellectual fabric of the university.

Subject Librarian Framework helps ensure that we provide a standard and equitable set of services to all departments. Two-way pipeline for communication.

Support for research, teaching, and learning. Establishes stronger ties between the library and the academic units. Aids in communicating the library's contribution to the university mission.

Support the university's academic mission to improve student experience and research outcomes. Dramatically increases the Libraries' visibility and collaboration with "new" areas and initiatives across campus. Liaison program facilitates the Libraries' ability to be a change agent across campus.

Supporting university mission. Make sure collections meet needs for research and teaching. Fulfillment that comes when librarians integrate into the research and learning community.

Various user groups have a primary point of contact in the library. Library is more responsive to user needs because of their partnerships and relationships. Raises our profile as active, engaged members of the campus community.

Visibility of library services and resources on campus. Increased usage of library resources and materials. Awareness of needs of stakeholders.

43. Please describe up to three top challenges for your library liaisons. N=61

Attracting and retaining language expertise.

Balancing workload both overall and within the number of departments a liaison is assigned to serve. Funding to support library initiatives that include participation and support by subject specialists. Better tracking and assessment of liaison activities, best practices, and effectiveness.

Balancing the needs of subject- and function-based expertise. Ensuring librarians have knowledge, expertise, skills needed for new liaison areas in a timely way.

Building relationships with busy faculty. Quantitative demand for teaching and consultation services. Broad range of subjects needing to be covered by a limited number of staff.

Challenge to balance the workload across liaisons (one big department versus many small departments—what is fair?). Challenge to liaisons in meeting the needs and demands among different disciplines. Challenge to communicate with other library departments about academic departmental needs.

Changing old habits (both staff and faculty) about library services. Difficult to provide pro-active service to all departments with existing staff. Greater importance of domain knowledge for liaisons; many support departments they do not have deep knowledge in.

Communication. Awareness by users. Consistency of service by all campus libraries.

Competing demands: Users expect quick response times for customer service vs. librarians' time needed for ongoing project management. Scale-up: Effective outreach can lead to challenging demands. Effectiveness and outcomes measures vary across disciplines. Identifying success measures is a challenge.

Convincing faculty and departments of liaison value. Coming up with the finances to purchase items liaisons request. Being able to hire and retain enough faculty to support a functional liaison program.

Departmental liaison only helps us understand individual faculty needs, and those often vary from the priorities of departments, divisions, and the VP/provostial level. Liaisons have varying skill levels, making it difficult for them to establish disciplinary credibility. Supervisors are frequently disengaged from liaison as a priority.

Despite our best efforts, not all campus programs, faculty, and students, take full advantage of liaison services. Data/ statistics keeping is time consuming and cumbersome.

Difficult to fulfill liaison duties in addition to other responsibilities. Some departments/schools could actually use more than one liaison.

Disinterested faculty, department heads, or deans. Varying size of departments can create workload issues. Too many departments for the number of liaisons.

Do not have enough people/librarians. Do not have enough time to accomplish all that could be done to support faculty and students. Do not have enough money to provide everything that faculty and students need.

Faculty & students are very busy. Financial constraints in the Libraries. Time constraints in the Libraries.

Faculty apathy. Closed communication of some departments (librarians not allowed to attend department meetings or post to email lists). Scale of audience.

Getting everyone up to speed on new services and documenting impact. Letting go of previous duties. Providing adequate support.

Getting the attention of faculty on library matters. Reaching the entire campus community. Keeping librarian skills relevant and current.

Having enough staff to match up with the large number of academic and administrative departments is challenging.

Inconsistent utilization of liaison services. Over-demand for specific specialized services. Cross-training.

Increasing workloads and needs for efficiently delivering services. Need to keep up with constantly changing landscape of scholarly communication. Interdisciplinary scholarship may require expertise in multiple subject areas.

Insufficient funds to provide all resources requested. More individuals are needed to support our current community, as well as new programs and faculty that are being introduced.

It's more difficult to get involved with some departments. Some are resistant to allowing librarians to speak at department meetings, be on listservs, etc. No budget for marketing. Librarians' lack of subject background in some disciplines.

Keeping up with demand for teaching. Finding balance between "traditional" services and new liaison roles. Establishing successful communication lines among distributed liaisons.

Lack of enough librarians to provide in-depth assistance. Thin coverage for extensive tasks, such as BI work with classes. Lack of response from some campus departments or faculty.

Lack of response or interest from busy faculty members. Time consuming for librarians, especially those assigned multiple departments. Difficulty understanding and meeting diverse needs of faculty.

Lack of subject and language expertise within the library adequate to cover all departments. Some liaisons doing work at a small percentage of their time. Not a primary role.

Lack of understanding of value of librarian work by university community. Lack of sufficient staff and expertise to cover all academic departments and research areas; this is very labor-intensive. Uneven skill sets and effort among liaisons.

Liaisons have multiple job responsibilities, so prioritizing is a challenge, and as a companion to this, not all librarians in our institution have liaison responsibilities, which may hinder the overall effectiveness of our program. Performance evaluation lines of responsibility. Liaisons have difficulty making time for continuing training given the pressure of multiple job responsibilities.

Liaisons understanding their roles and adapting to them. Dynamic landscape. Change in personnel throughout the campus.

Low staffing; spread too thin. Hard to convey importance of activities to library management. Lack of marketing and technology support to evolve services.

Making sure every department has a liaison. Not overloading a liaison. Replacing a liaison who has multiple departmental assignments.

Meeting diverse disciplinary needs for liaison services. Managing individual liaison workloads. Balancing traditional and emerging services.

Meeting the diverse needs of a large campus community. Assessing the effectiveness of the liaison services offered. Making the students and faculty aware of the services offered by liaison librarians.

More requests and opportunities than staff can handle. No additional funding to support program. Users who are more aware of resources request more than library can afford.

Moving from if-you-build-it-they-will-come support model to outreach-focused partner model. Finding ways to scale liaison services with shrinking staff and constantly changing needs. Balancing traditional liaison skills with new academic needs.

Not all departments participate. Victims of our success so not enough liaisons. Some liaisons focus too much in one area such as collections or instruction and need better distribution of services.

Not all liaisons are as proactive in service development as they could be. Workforce development to address the changing needs can be a challenge.

Not enough liaisons to satisfy the needs of all faculties and departments across campus. Difficulty in giving up or stopping some services. Creating a common focus/vision for the liaison program.

People. Time. Money.

Providing high quality resources with stressed budgets. Time management of liaisons' competing responsibilities. Finding the best ways to communicate with faculty in other colleges.

Recruitment and retention of qualified staff. Insuring that institutional service standards are met. Achievement of successful engagements with academic departments.

Reframing the role of the liaison to academic departments. Faculty who insist on print rather than e-books. Liaisons must be able to build relationships and have to get out of the library and into the departments.

Relationship building and true collaboration is hard and time-consuming. Lack of agreement among liaison librarians of the value of the work. Work is amorphous and ambiguous and relies on opportunity and individual relationships.

Requires continuous effort to engage with changing populations with a variety of communication preferences. Faculty clients, particularly, are very busy with many demands on their time. Building and maintaining necessary skill sets in a time of rapid change (technology, data science & management, etc.) Determining appropriate quantitative and qualitative measure of liaison's activity and outcomes.

Resistance to change in duties from library liaisons. Reaching departments that are not overly-receptive to liaison services.

Responsiveness of departments. Breadth and depth of possible engagements (both in terms of topics and methods). Time.

Scalability. Balancing workload. Buy in from librarians too embedded in departments.

Scalability and resource allocations. How do we measure success and outcomes. Communications from and to liaisons.

Size of departments/colleges assigned to just one liaison. Sustainability of services/availability given the liaison-to-student or faculty member ratio. Balancing outward-focused liaison services with the work of the organization/projects/initiatives.

Some departments aren't very responsive, and many faculty do not consider it essential. We can't serve everyone—sometimes we have more demand than we can meet. We have both funding and staffing issues. It is difficult to coordinate liaison services across subject areas.

Some departments more communicative than others about their needs.

Some liaisons are more engaged than others. Using liaisons to communicate with faculty can result in uneven distribution of information. Keeping liaisons abreast of trends in new areas: data management, scholarly communications, demand driven acquisitions, etc.

Some liaisons need more training to learn how to provide user-based services. The workload of liaisons is increasingly heavy; not enough time to do all of the work. Paradigm shift is necessary to focus more on what users want and less on what librarians do.

Sufficient time/staff to be as creative and responsive as we would like. Sufficient time to develop expertise in multiple disciplines. Perception by some academic departments that they are self-sufficient.

The changing research and publishing landscape requires new skills and attitudes that not all liaisons currently have. Faculty do not understand what libraries do and are confused about liaison roles and services. The problem of liaisons focusing on what they do rather than on the impacts they make.

The more popular liaison services become the harder it is to meet all of the needs/collaborate with everyone who is interested. Victims of our own success. Finding ways to make liaison services relevant and appealing to those units that have not yet taken advantage of these services.

Time. Lack of people. Lack of ability/money to provide what faculty need/want.

Time intensive. Difficult to scale—some departments are big, meaning that some liaisons have a lot of departments. Difficult to evaluate—hard to determine what success looks like for different departments.

Uneven level of support provided. May have expertise in one area and less in another (i.e., instruction vs. collection management).

Workload & staffing levels with new programs and no increase in library resources. Receptivity of some departments to liaison involvement. Keeping up-to-date on emerging areas such as scholarly communication, research support, bibliometrics, etc.

ADDITIONAL COMMENTS

44. **Please enter any additional information regarding liaison services at your library that may assist the authors in accurately analyzing the results of this survey.** N=18

Coming out of a reorganization. New liaison program is just starting this fall. Focused on engagement, communication, outreach. Liaisons not expected to meet all departmental needs themselves but to leverage the diverse strengths of the newly formed library teams.

In addition to liaisons we do have a Director of Communications and Outreach who responds to all emails coming in to the general library email address of the webpage. She also handles general library messaging, media relations, social media activity, and marketing campaigns. She supervises a student liaison, who is a student working 1/2 time who is generally tasked with collecting feedback and representing student perspectives in library decision making. Ideally, we'd like to have one for undergraduate students and one for graduate students. At present we only have one position.

In the University Libraries we feel our liaisons are more important than ever in the work we are doing to support campus priorities and strategic directions. The liaison's deep subject knowledge and strong relationships with faculty are leading to interesting projects and opportunities for collaboration between the faculty and the library.

In the last 5–10 years, librarians have made deliberate efforts to move away from a "bibliographer" model (which tended to emphasize selection of materials for the collection) and toward offering expertise-based support to help students and researchers find, interact with, transform, and use materials in our collections. This now includes areas such as managing and manipulating data and digital texts, and advice on issues in scholarly publishing and copyright.

Liaisons in our library offer different levels of services beyond the core responsibilities, based on their skills, experience, and comfort level. Members of all academic departments have access to the full menu of services, such as instruction and research consultations, but in some cases they are provided by a reference & instruction librarian instead of the specific departmental liaison.

Librarians with data management/e-science, data sets/data librarian, GIS/remote sensing, IP/scholarly communication, and repository expertise are not within the subject librarian org structure. However, we work closely with offices. Subject librarians serve on committees for each of these areas, and we refer people as needed.

One challenge in the coming year will be to review the liaisons' roles in collection development, and to encourage more outward-facing engagement with our community. We will be exploring ways to do this in the coming year. Also, regarding the question about goals, individual liaisons set goals as part of their overall goal setting at the beginning of each evaluation year; these are set in consultation with their director supervisor(s). The maximum number of departments that are assigned to one liaison is approximate, as some liaisons have programs and inter-disciplinary institutes assigned to them, others are curators of collections. Also note that this does not apply to the non-academic portion of the answers above, as those assignments are currently with a few number of librarians.

Our liaison has been unstructured and free form. We plan this year to appoint a position to coordinate liaison services. This individual will be responsible for creating and implementing a formal program.

Thanks for this survey. Lots of interesting questions here!! Apologies for not being able to answer so many of them!! I think that many of the answers to these questions are somewhat nuanced, particularly given the degree of variability across units, and across individual approaches to liaison roles.

The Associate Dean, Research Services, position coordinates the liaisons, leads twice monthly meetings, and heads the CD Committee.

The extent to which liaisons embrace and offer expanded roles or new things (such as data management, metrics and impact training, etc.) varies widely across the Libraries. More changes are coming, including de-emphasis of title-by-title selection, which challenges some liaisons given that their careers and professional identities are associated with the (largely print) collections they've built and maintain.

The role of the Personal Librarian (liaison) evolves as each librarian seeks ways to best meet the needs of the faculty and students in their subject areas.

This is a very recent shift, approximately four months into organizational restructuring. It would help to have ARL standards and guidelines and models and benchmarks for liaison work so that we could have some standardization among the ARLs.

We are currently reviewing and recasting our liaison program to focus specifically on the scholarly engine at the university, that is, the processes of research and knowledge creation that result in the production of, dissemination of, preservation of, and access to our scholarly output.

We are just beginning work on formalizing expectations and evaluation of liaison services. It would be interesting to see where we are in a year or two.

We have a number of functional specialists, not subject-based, that provide support to our faculty and other community members. Examples are our copyright and licensing librarian and the head of our scholarly communication center.

We have found that librarians who come in with a great deal of subject expertise in the disciplines of their assigned departments are better able to gain the trust of the faculty and to integrate and collaborate within their assigned departments. The trend for us has been to hire liaison librarians with deep subject knowledge, and they obtain the MLS after being hired.

We were an early adopter of liaison services, and for the most part have kept up with the changing scholarly communication landscape in order to work effectively with faculty. Because we have a separate data management services unit that reports to the director of our entrepreneurial library program, we have been less active in that area. Liaisons connect faculty to that staff and provide basic information on data management.

RESPONDING INSTITUTIONS

University of Alberta

Boston Public Library

Boston University

Brigham Young University

University of Calgary

University of California, Irvine

University of California, Los Angeles

University of California, San Diego

Case Western Reserve University

University of Colorado at Boulder

Colorado State University

Columbia University

University of Connecticut

Cornell University

Duke University

Emory University

University of Florida

Florida State University

George Washington University

Georgetown University

University of Georgia

University of Guelph

University of Hawaii at Manoa

University of Houston

University of Illinois at Chicago

Indiana University Bloomington

University of Iowa

Iowa State University

Johns Hopkins University

University of Kentucky

Library of Congress

University of Louisville

McGill University

McMaster University

University of Maryland

University of Massachusetts, Amherst

University of Michigan

Michigan State University

University of Missouri

National Library of Medicine

New York University

University of North Carolina at Chapel Hill

North Carolina State University

Northwestern University

Ohio University

Ohio State University

University of Oklahoma

Oklahoma State University

University of Oregon

University of Pennsylvania

Pennsylvania State University

Purdue University

Rutgers University

University of South Carolina

University of Southern California

Southern Illinois University Carbondale

Stony Brook University, SUNY

Syracuse University

Temple University

University of Texas at Austin

Texas A&M University

Texas Tech University

University of Toronto

Vanderbilt University

University of Virginia

Virginia Tech

University of Washington

Washington University in St. Louis

University of Waterloo

Yale University

REPRESENTATIVE DOCUMENTS

Liaison Services

CASE WESTERN RESERVE UNIVERSITY

CASE WESTERN RESERVE UNIVERSITY
Librarian/Faculty Liaison Program
http://library.case.edu/ksl/services/research/rsl/

Summon: Search across the library's collections…

Search Summon

or access the Advanced Search Catalog Databases or eJournals directly

HOME
COLLECTIONS
SERVICES
FACILITIES
GIVE TO THE
LIBRARY
ABOUT US

Librarian/Faculty Liaison Program

The *Librarian/Faculty Liaison Program* provides faculty with an ongoing opportunity to keep abreast of KSL services and collections. Each academic department has a designated research services librarian who maintains an awareness of the department's research and teaching needs. Departments are encouraged to include their librarian in meetings, research projects, and other activities, especially when library support is a factor to be considered. Librarians also teach classes related to research and information retrieval. We would be happy to develop a course-related instruction component for any of your classes. These classes, one or several, focus on specific research databases and other resources that students may use to for papers and projects. For more information, contact a librarian listed below.

KSL also strongly encourages each department to formally designate a faculty member as the department's library liaison so that communication remains current. The department's liaison should keep the department informed of library activities and will act as the primary contact and advocate for faculty representing the needs of the department to the library.

Case School of Engineering
- **Biomedical Engineering** - Daniela Solomon, daniela.solomon2@case.edu, 368-8790
- **Chemical & Biomolecular Engineering** - Brian C. Gray, brian.c.gray@case.edu, 368-8685
- **Civil Engineering** - Daniela Solomon, daniela.solomon2@case.edu, 368-8790
- **Electrical Engineering & Computer Science** - Daniela Solomon, daniela.solomon2@case.edu, 368-8790
- **Macromolecular Science & Engineering** - Brian C. Gray, brian.c.gray@case.edu, 368-8685
- **Materials Science & Engineering** - Daniela Solomon, daniela.solomon2@case.edu, 368-8790
- **Mechanical & Aerospace Engineering** - Daniela Solomon, daniela.solomon2@case.edu, 368-8790

College of Arts and Sciences
- **Anthropology** - Karen Thornton, karen.thornton@case.edu, 368-6511
- **Art History and Art** - Leigh Bonds, leigh.bonds@case.edu, 368-4253
- **Astronomy** - Karen Thornton, karen.thornton@case.edu, 368-6511
- **Biology** - Yuening Zhang, yuening.zhang@case.edu, 368-5310
- **Chemistry** - Yuening Zhang, yuening.zhang@case.edu, 368-5310
- **Classics** - Stephen Toombs, stephen.toombs@case.edu, 368-2403
- **Cognitive Science** - Karen Thornton, karen.thornton@case.edu, 368-6511
- **Dance** - Stephen Toombs, stephen.toombs@case.edu, 368-2403
- **English** - William Claspy, william.claspy@case.edu, 368-3595
- **Earth, Environmental, & Planetary Sciences (Geology)** - Evan Meszaros, evan.meszaros@case.edu, 368-3509
- **History** - William Claspy, william.claspy@case.edu, 368-3595
- **Mathematics, Applied Mathematics, & Statistics** - Karen Thornton, karen.thornton@case.edu, 368-6511
- **Modern Languages & Literature** - William Claspy, william.claspy@case.edu, 368-3595
- **Music** - Stephen Toombs, stephen.toombs@case.edu, 368-2403
- **Philosophy** - Karen Thornton, karen.thornton@case.edu, 368-6511
- **Physics** - Yuening Zhang, yuening.zhang@case.edu, 368-5310
- **Political Science** - Mark Eddy, mark.eddy@case.edu, 368-5457
- **Psychological Sciences** - Mark Eddy, mark.eddy@case.edu, 368-5457
- **Religious Studies** - Mark Eddy, mark.eddy@case.edu, 368-5457
- **Sociology** - Mark Eddy, mark.eddy@case.edu, 368-5457
- **Theatre** - Stephen Toombs, stephen.toombs@case.edu, 368-2403

Weatherhead School of Management
Karen Oye, karen.oye@case.edu, 368-5309

- **Accountancy**
- **Banking & Finance**
- **Design & Innovation**
- **Economics**
- **Operations**
- **Organizational Behavior**

Interdisciplinary Areas

Main Library / LibGuides / Subject Librarians / Liaisons at Emory

Subject Librarians: Liaisons at Emory

Identifies who we are and what we do

| Search |

Liaisons at Emory | **TaskForce & Team Leader Documentation**

Liaison Roles Documentation

- ☐ Subject Librarian Roles & Responsibilities (current version)
  Written by a diverse team of librarians after reviewing our peers and results of library focus groups and surveys of Emory faculty and students. Approved July 2013 by the Senior Vice Provost for Library Services while serving as the interim Director of Libraries.

- ☐ Liaison Roles 2009 version
  The Division changed leadership and teams were changed. Likewise, the ARL Liaison report was used to update our roles.

- ☐ Liaison Roles 2004 version
  Teams were consolidated and the document was changed to reflect this. Library Administration approved changes in 2004.

- ☐ Liaison Roles 2002 version
  The original document when subject liaisons were first implemented and assigned at Woodruff Library

Emory Liaisons

Contacting Subject Librarians is possible from several links at the Woodruff Library.

Meet our Subject Liaisons Directory

Consultation Services

Library Instruction

Class Research Guides

Ask a librarian

Purchase Request

Collection Policies

SL Training Materials

- ☐ Recording SL stats via Desktracker
- Collection Management Team
- ☐ Suggestions for Training & Professional Development

Defining a SL

A subject librarian provides the full range of subject specific library services to the academic department, including collection management, consultation, instruction, assessment, and reference. The subject librarian maintains and expands research-level collections, acts as an expert guide, provides research help at the time of need, and contributes to the programmatic and collaborative work of the Services Division and the library in general.

Recent Emory Liaison Job Descriptions

- ☐ Humanities Librarian
  2015 opening
- ☐ Social Sciences Librarian
  2015 opening
- ☐ Science Librarian
  Chemistry & Physics 2014
- ☐ Humanities Librarian
  2010 position
- ☐ Social Sciences Librarian/ Psych
  2010 position

Additional Materials

- ☐ Subject Liaison Roles and Skills, Bryson
  Constellation of subject liaison duties.
- ☐ Subject Liaison Roles and Skills with Graphic, Bryson

Additional Readings from other Universities

- Duke Libraries
- University of Minnesota Libraries
- ARL 2009 Liaison Report

Home	Services	Collections	Health Sciences

About Us | My Account | Disability Services | Mobile

Ask a Librarian | Site search | Go

UNIVERSITY LIBRARY
UIC

Find
Books
Articles
Journals
Databases A - Z
Research and Subject Guides
Dictionaries and more
Course Reserves
Newspapers

Locations
Richard J. Daley Library
Health Sciences - Chicago
Health Sciences - Peoria
Health Sciences - Rockford
Health Sciences - Urbana

Other Topics
UIC Library Dashboard
Giving to the Library

Book a Study Room
Library Events

Connect with us

You are here: Home » About Us » Departmental Liaisons

About Us
Contact Us
Departmental Liaisons
Employment
Giving to the Library
Hours
Library Faculty Research
Library Policies
Library/IT Assessment
Locations
Mission and Profile
News and Events
Staff Directory
UIC Library Dashboard

Departmental Liaisons

About the liaison program

The University Library has appointed a *liaison librarian* for each department. Liaison librarians offer a number of services including:

- presentations at orientation events, departmental meetings, or other forums
- reference services that encompass one-on-one consultations for you and your students
- course-related library instruction
- review of recommendations to add to the Library's electronic and print collections
- partnership on E-scholarship efforts that include data curation and preservation
- information on scholarly communication initiatives.

- East Side / Daley Library Liaisons
- Campus-Wide Services Liaisons
- LHS – Chicago Liaisons
- LHS – Peoria Liaisons
- LHS – Rockford Liaisons
- LHS – Urbana Liaisons

East Side / Daley Library Liaison Affiliations and Contact Information

College	Liaison	Departments
Architecture, Design and the Arts	Jane Darcovich (312) 413-7677 darcovic@uic.edu	Architecture; Art and Art History; Design
Architecture, Design and the Arts	John Cullars (312) 413-0020 jcullars@uic.edu	Theatre and Music
Business Administration	Marcia Dellenbach (312) 413-3045 dellenba@uic.edu	Accounting; Information and Decision Sciences Managerial Studies
Business Administration	Glenda Insua (312) 996-4032 ginsua1@uic.edu	Finance
CUPPA	John Shuler (312) 413-2594 alfred@uic.edu	All departments
Education	Annie Armstrong (312) 413-3045 annie@uic.edu	All departments
Engineering	David Dror (312) 996-1886 ddror@uic.edu	All departments
Liberal Arts and Sciences	Catherine Lantz (312) 996-6633 clantz@uic.edu	Biological sciences; Chemistry; Earth and Environmental Sciences
Liberal Arts and Sciences	David Dror (312) 996-1886 ddror@uic.edu	Mathematics, Statistics, and Computer Science; Physics
Liberal Arts and Sciences	Glenda Insua (312) 996-4032 ginsua1@uic.edu	Economics
Liberal Arts and Sciences	Annie Armstrong (312) 413-3045 annie@uic.edu	Psychology

UNIVERSITY
LIBRARIES

Search the UMD Libraries website

Monday, October 5, 2015
McKeldin — Open 24 hours. Ending Friday at 8pm
Art — 09:00AM - 08:00PM
Architecture — 02:00PM - 07:00PM
Chemistry — 08:00AM - 10:00PM
EPSL — 08:00AM - 11:00PM
Media Services in Hornbake — 08:00AM - 10:00PM
Special Collections in Hornbake — 10:00AM - 05:00PM
MSPAL — 08:30AM - 11:00PM
Shady Grove — See here for hours

Services

▶ Access, Borrow, Request
▶ Computing
▶ Copy, Print, Scan
▶ Course Reserves
▶ Disabilities Services
▶ Equipment for Loan
▶ Federal Depository Program
▶ For Faculty & Grads
▶ Interlibrary Loan / UBorrow
▶ Open Access
▶ Research Data Services
▶ Reserve a Room or Carrel
▶ Suggest a Purchase
▶ Terrapin Learning Commons
▶ Research Commons
▶ Teaching & Learning Services
▶ Use a Library Computer

Library Liaison System

The Library Liaison System at the University of Maryland exists to establish ongoing relationships between the UMD Libraries and the University's academic departments. At its core, The Library Liaison System is composed of subject librarians and departmental faculty. These Library Liaisons and Departmental Liaisons work together to enhance communication and improve library resources and services.

GUIDELINES

Guidelines for Subject Librarian Liaisons

Guidelines for Departmental Liaisons

EMAIL REFLECTORS (@UMD.EDU)

Library Liaison Reflector: **sel-liaison**

Departmental Liaison Reflector: **libdeptliaisons**

LIAISON LISTS & CONTACT INFORMATION

Librarian Subject Specialists (Directory of)

Departmental Liaisons

Last update: Jul 23, 2012
Questions? Contact us.

DOCUMENTS

○ Liaison System Update to University Library Council (March 6, 2009)
○ Liaison System Implementation Group, Final Report (January 16, 2009)
○ Liaison System Working Group, Final Report (May 22, 2007)
○ University Library Council, Report on Liaison System (April 2006)

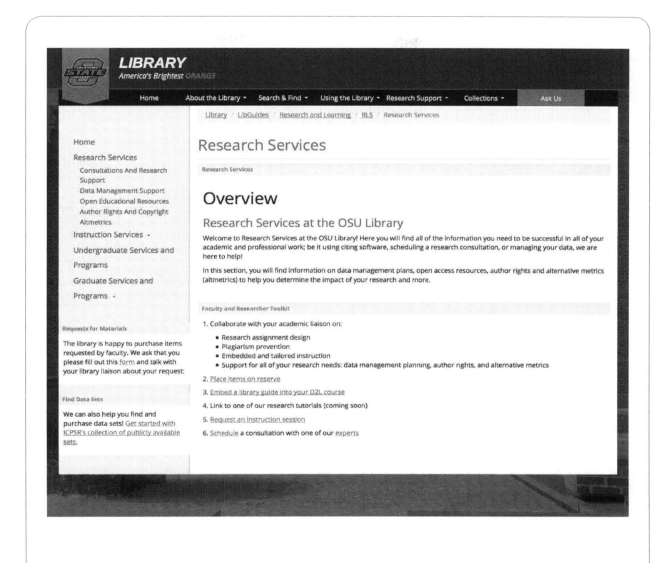

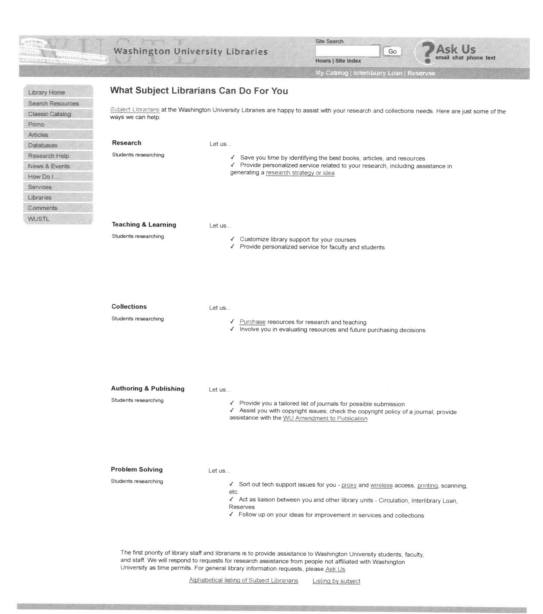

Position Descriptions

Libraries & Information Technology Human Resources

Professional Position Posting

Humanities Librarian, English Literature

Department: Emory Libraries, Humanities Team

Salary: Commensurate with qualifications and experience

Position Availability: Immediately

The Emory Libraries seek an energetic, user-oriented, and collaborative professional to serve as a Humanities Librarian on the Humanities Team with a subject area focus of English Literature. Emory's well-ranked and dynamic English department includes 40 faculty, over 50 graduate students, and more than 150 undergraduate majors. The successful candidate will be highly knowledgeable in the field of English and American Literature, have a passion for the research, teaching and learning mission of the University, and understand the Libraries' role in the advancement of that mission. S/he will possess excellent communication, interpersonal, and team skills. This position offers an opportunity for strategic and interdisciplinary approaches to the selection, teaching, discovery, and delivery of digital and print information resources.

<u>**Position Duties**</u>

Reporting to the Humanities Team Leader, the Humanities Librarian will be involved and engaged in the entire life-cycle of research, teaching and learning processes. S/he will collaborate with and support faculty in course-specific ways, including providing point-of-need instruction sessions and assignments, research guides and/or tutorials. Focused primarily on the English department, the librarian will provide a full range of subject specific library services to include collection development, consultation, instruction, reference services, and assessment. The librarian will also work closely with other librarians and units to understand and integrate area research and curricular needs with the Libraries' collections and services. Partnering with fellow subject librarians, other Library & Information Technology Services (LITS) units, and campus organizations, the Humanities Librarian will work to create and sustain strong relationships with the Manuscript, Archives, & Rare Book Library (MARBL), Emory's Center for Digital Scholarship (ECDS), and Academic Technology Services to engage in evolving campus digital scholarship initiatives. Finally, s/he also will work the reference desk an average of 3 hours a week. Specific duties include:

- Serves as primary liaison to and actively develops professional relationships with faculty, students and staff in assigned subject area. May include other areas within the Humanities Team if needed.
- Plans and delivers innovative reference and instruction services; teaches research tools and skills relevant to the discipline, develops content for subject-based web pages, and collaborates with faculty to achieve information and digital literacies and archival pedagogy learning outcomes in course-specific ways.
- Provides in-depth, specialized consultation in support of the entire research lifecycle; contributes to University efforts to assess and promote institutional scholarship.
- Assists faculty engaged in digital scholarship projects and teaching-and-learning-with-technology initiatives; collaborates as needed with ECDS and Academic Technology Services.
- Partners with other libraries, especially research services in MARBL, to promote teaching and research with primary evidence materials.
- Develops and manages excellent electronic, multimedia, and print collections in English and American literature to support the research and teaching needs of the Emory University community, promotes resources using current tools and technologies, and collaborates with colleagues in related fields to acquire materials, especially the curators in MARBL.

- Provides marketing and assessment of library services.
- Participates in professional and scholarly associations.
- Maintains up-to-date professional knowledge and skills in areas related to primary job assignment as well as maintains general knowledge of current trends in higher education, academic libraries, and information and educational technology.
- Adheres to guidelines outlined in the *Handbook Governing the Librarian series for Faculty-Equivalent Librarians* to ensure appointment, appointment renewal and promotion-in-rank
- Participates in library and campus committees as appropriate for service purposes.

Required Qualifications
- ALA-accredited master's degree in Library and Information Science or equivalent education and experience (subject expertise).
- Advanced degree in English Literature or related discipline.
- Demonstrated knowledge and experience with instruction, information literacy, and assessment of library services and resources.
- Familiarity with new technologies, such as text-mining, network analysis, data-visualization, and other digital applications relevant to the study of English literature.
- Commitment to user-centered library services.
- Strong interest in technology and tools for research and teaching
- Strong understanding of the key issues and trends in instruction, collection development, research, and reference in the subject area of English.
- Knowledge of scholarly communication issues and trends within the literature disciplines.
- Evidence of excellent communication, public speaking, teaching, writing and analytical skills.
- Commitment to fostering a diverse educational environment and workplace and an ability to work effectively with a diverse faculty, staff, and student population.
- Demonstrated willingness to respond to new opportunities with initiative, creative energy, and leadership.
- Evidence of active participation, involvement, and leadership in local, state, regional, national, or international professional or scholarly associations.

Preferred Qualifications
- Practical knowledge of ACRL's Framework for Information Literacy for Higher Education.
- Experience working with Aleph, ALMA, vendor sites, like YBP's GOBI, libguides, LibAnswers, and other assessment tools.
- Background and/or interest in other humanities disciplines, such as comparative literature or classics.

Application Procedures
Interested candidates should review the applications requirements and apply online at
https://sjobs.brassring.com/1033/ASP/TG/cim_jobdetail.asp?partnerid=25066&siteid=5449&areq=53093br

Applications may be submitted as Word or PDF attachments and must include:

    1) Cover letter of application describing qualifications and experience;
    2) Current resume/vita detailing education and relevant experience; and
    3) On a separate document list the names, email addresses, and telephone numbers of 3 professional references including a current or previous supervisor.

Candidates applying by June 26, 2015 will receive priority consideration. Review of applications will continue until position is successfully filled. Emory is an Equal Opportunity/Affirmative Action Employer that welcomes and encourages diversity and seeks applications and nominations from women and minorities.

<u>**General Information**</u>

Professional librarians at Emory Libraries are 12-month faculty-equivalent positions evaluated annually with assigned ranks renewable for 3 or 5 years based on experience and background. Appropriate professional leave and funding is provided. Depending on educational credentials and position, librarians may be considered for a shared/dual appointment between the library and academic department as a faculty member.

Librarian appointees at Emory generally have educational credentials and professional backgrounds with academic library experience and/or disciplinary knowledge and demonstrate a commitment to continuous learning, professional engagement and involvement, research and scholarship, creativity, innovation, and flexibility. Such backgrounds will normally include a graduate degree from an ALA-accredited library and information science program AND/OR a discipline-specific master's OR doctoral degree. In addition to professional competence and service within the library in the primary job assignment, advancement and/or appointment renewal requires professional involvement and contributions outside of the library and scholarly activities. Candidates must show evidence or promise of such contributions.

Emory provides an extremely competitive fringe benefit plan that includes personal leave, holiday pay, medical and dental plans, life insurance, courtesy scholarships, and tuition reimbursement just to name a few. For a full list of benefit programs, please go to http://www.hr.emory.edu/eu/benefits/.

<u>**Description of Institution and Library**</u>

Emory University is internationally recognized for its outstanding liberal arts college, superb professional schools, and one of the South's leading health care systems. Emory's beautiful, leafy main campus is located in Atlanta's historic Druid Hills suburb and is home to 7,836 undergraduates and 6,677 graduate and professional students. As the third largest private employer in Atlanta, Emory University and Emory Healthcare have a combined workforce of approximately, 27,937 and an annual operating budget of $4.3 billion. Emory University received $507.1 million in research funding in 2013. Emory recently concluded a successful fundraising campaign that raised $1.69 billion from 149,000 donors.

Ranked among the top 25 Association of Research Libraries (ARL) in North America, Emory University Libraries in Atlanta and Oxford, Georgia are an intellectual commons for Emory University. Comprised of 9 libraries, the holdings include more than 3.9 million print and electronic volumes, 83,000-plus electronic journals, and internationally renowned special collections. Emory is well known in a number of collection areas including modern literature, African-American history and culture, U.S. Southern history and culture, and U.S. civil rights. Emory Libraries staff number approximately 137 and the overall library budget is approximately $25.3 million. The Emory Libraries is a member of the Association of Research Libraries (ARL), the Coalition for Networked Information (CNI), the Center for Research Libraries (CRL), the Council on Library and Information Resources (CLIR), the Digital Library Federation (DLF), International Federation of Library Associations and Institutions (IFLA), and the Scholarly Publishing & Academic Resources Coalition (SPARC) as well as regional associations including the Association of Southeastern Research Libraries (ASERL), Georgia Library Learning Online (GALILEO), and the GETSM Consortium (a consortium of the University of Georgia, Emory, Georgia Tech, Georgia State University, and Georgia Regents University).

The Emory Libraries include the Robert W. Woodruff Library, which is also home to the MARBL. Other campus libraries, which serve the specialized and professional schools, include the Goizueta Business Library, the Woodruff Health Sciences Library, the Pitts Theology Library and the Hugh F. MacMillan Law Library in addition to the Oxford College Library located on the Oxford Campus approximately 30 miles from Atlanta.

– 18 July 2014

EEO/AA/Disability/Veteran Employer

Clinical Services Librarian

Clinical services librarians at the University of Louisville (UofL) Kornhauser Health Sciences Library serve as an information expert for clinical departments and researchers including their staff, residents, faculty, attending physicians, nurses and students.

Responsibilities include:

- Serving as a clinical librarian embedded within clinical departments
- Engaging with users in their preferred environments, typically outside the library
- Building a collaborative relationship within clinical departments to support information literacy and evidence based practice
- Actively participating in hospital rounds, morning report and evidence- based healthcare teaching sessions
- Collaborating with clinical faculty, residents or students on journal clubs, seminars, systematic literature review projects, and other clinical forums
- Providing immediate information as requested using current technology and resources
- Keeping students, faculty, and staff in touch with emerging technologies and electronic information tools in the field of medicine
- Participating in the development of the Kornhauser Health Sciences Library's clinical library services program
- Participating in the management of the library
- Providing service at library information desk
- Engaging in scholarship and activity in appropriate professional organizations

Required Qualifications

- Master's degree from an ALA-accredited program or international equivalent in library or information science
- Excellent presentation and relationship building skills
- Ability to think and react quickly in an intense clinical environment
- Experience using biomedical and evidence based practice literature, research, and clinical tools
- Demonstrated ability to learn and use new technologies
- Demonstrated ability to communicate effectively in multiple formats to diverse audiences
- Demonstrated evidence of initiative and flexibility with planning and problem-solving
- Proven ability to work creatively, collaboratively and effectively as both a team member and independently
- Demonstrated commitment to health sciences librarianship
- Potential to meet promotion and tenure requirements

Desirable Qualifications

- Experience working with users in their environments, as opposed to traditional library services
- Understanding of evidence-based practice
- Experience in a health sciences library
- Experience using EndNote or similar citation management software
- Health sciences background
- Additional graduate degree or certification in a related discipline

POSITION DESCRIPTION

Working Title: Global Public Health Librarian

Supervisor: Kate McGraw, Assist. Depart. Head for User Services   Date Completed: May 5, 2015

Primary purpose of position:

The Librarian will provide client-centered information and education services using a variety of methods and technologies with a primary focus on serving researchers, faculty, students and staff in the Gillings School of Global Public Health. Work is performed in client settings and in the library. Information services are provided through office hours in the school, consultations, chat, email, telephone, and the User Services Center. Education services are provided by offering curriculum integrated instruction and by developing online user guides and tutorials. The person in this position will also contribute to the Health Sciences Library's Global Engagement initiatives and work with the Area Health Education Centers staff to meet the needs of public health practitioners and students across the state.

Principal responsibilities:

- Initiate relationships with researchers, faculty, staff, and students working in cross-disciplinary public health courses, programs, centers, and institutes (both on and off campus) to identify and fulfill needs for information and education services.
- Maintain current knowledge and share expertise in searching the wide range of information tools used in public health, particularly in the areas of global health, health statistics and informatics.
- Maintain and share knowledge of innovative information, education and communication methods and tools, especially as they relate to public health practice.
- Develop an understanding of the research themes important to the School and identify ways the Library can support and partner with public health researchers.
- Actively develop local, regional, national and international collaborations to advance the strategic directions and Global Engagement initiatives of the Library.
- Pursue research and professional development activities appropriate to maintaining or advancing appointment rank.

REQUIRED Knowledge, Skills and Abilities:
- ALA-accredited Master's degree in library or information science.
- Minimum two years of experience as a health sciences librarian or comparable work providing health information services.
- Ability to demonstrate knowledge of public health information sources and how they are used in public health education, research and practice.
- Ability to provide and assess information competency instruction for both in-person and distance education students.
- Excellent oral and written communication skills.
- Flexible self-starter with demonstrated ability to discover and use innovative approaches.
- Ability to work effectively and collaboratively with diverse colleagues, students, faculty, and researchers.
- Demonstrated commitment to continued professional development.

PREFERRED Knowledge, Skills and Abilities:
- Public health education or work experience.
- Knowledge of the systematic review process.

- Experience partnering with researchers conducting systematic reviews.
- Current experience using instructional technology tools for distance education.
- Experience finding funding opportunities or writing grants.
- Experience using EndNote, RefWorks and similar products.
- Experience developing online content using web tools such as LibGuides, blogs, wikis, MOOCs.

FIND (//WWW.LIB.NCSU.EDU/FIND)

HOME (/)   JOBS (/JOBS)   EPA (/JOBS/EPA)   VACANCY ANNOUNCEMENT: RESEARCH LIBRARIAN FOR ENGINEERING AND BIOTECHNOLOGY

Vacancy Announcement: Research Librarian for Engineering and Biotechnology

NORTH CAROLINA STATE UNIVERSITY LIBRARIES

VACANCY ANNOUNCEMENT

RESEARCH LIBRARIAN FOR ENGINEERING AND BIOTECHNOLOGY

The NCSU Libraries has a well-earned reputation for creating adventurous library spaces and innovative services that delight today's students and researchers. The award-winning James B. Hunt Jr. Library (/huntlibrary), opened in 2013 on NC State's Centennial Campus (http://centennial.ncsu.edu), offers faculty and students access to advanced technologies such as large-scale visualization, simulated environments, 3D imagery, and interactive computing that are enabling revolutionary ways to see and use information. An iconic building that captures NC State's spirit of innovation in education and research, the Hunt Library is recognized as one of the world's most creative learning and collaborative spaces and a model for "the library of the future". The D. H. Hill Library, serving the main campus, combines the best of tradition and innovation, housing special collections and a beautiful gallery alongside vibrant, experiential spaces such as the Learning Commons, Technology Sandbox, Visualization Studio, and Makerspace. If you are a person who would like to provide a new generation of library users with everything they can imagine and more, consider applying for this position.

The NCSU Libraries invites applications and nominations for the **Research Librarian for Engineering and Biotechnology**. NCSU research librarians collaborate actively with faculty members, students, and researchers, supporting their disciplinary and interdisciplinary research and scholarship across its life cycle and offering expertise in emerging technologies; data science, analytics, and management; and visualization. NC State University has made a strategic investment in supporting interdisciplinary research by establishing the Chancellor's Faculty Excellence Program (/faculty-clusters), a "faculty cluster" initiative to address major global challenges. Many of the 20 cluster themes involve engineering and the biosciences. Reporting to the Director of Centennial Campus Research Services and based in the James B. Hunt Jr. Library, this position supports research and teaching in interdisciplinary areas such as biomedical engineering, biotextiles, bioinformatics, and translational regenerative medicine.

Responsibilities

The Research Librarian for Engineering and Biotechnology:

> Performs outreach to engage faculty throughout the life cycle of research and teaching.

> Provides research consultation services for faculty and students.

> Supports and enables faculty and students in the use of data analysis, visualization applications, and technology-rich library spaces such as visualization labs.

> Supports data management needs of researchers.

Human Resources department at the University of Waterloo

Liaison Librarian

Date:	June 26, 2014
Reports to (Job Title):	Head, Information Services and Resources (ISR), Dana Porter Library or Head, Information Services and Resources (ISR), Davis Centre
Jobs Reporting (Job Titles):	None
Location:	Library Main Campus, Optometry, or Pharmacy
Grade:	USG 8 - 13 35 hr/wk

Primary Purpose

Liaison Librarians are the Library's primary contact with the University's Schools/Academic Departments. Each Liaison Librarian is a member of the Information Services and Resources Department and is responsible for one or more Academic Department/School. Liaison Librarians enhance the Library's contribution to the University community through the development and delivery of library information services and resources to faculty members, students and staff.

In order to support research, teaching and learning at the University of Waterloo, Liaison Librarians are proactive in information resources development and management as well as the development and provision of instructional activities that support the curriculum and develop students' research related literacies and lifelong learning. As appropriate, the Liaison Librarians contribute expertise in support of grant applications and the research process. Librarians are knowledgeable of, and engaged in activities related to scholarly research, inquiry, and publishing.

Liaison Librarians work closely with Library departments, committees, and others as appropriate to advance the Library's strategic directions and lead projects and initiatives in their areas of responsibility and expertise.

Key Accountabilities:

1.	As a Liaison Librarian, the incumbent:
	• Supports and advances the Library's strategic directions to further the Library's contribution to the campus Strategic Plan for learning, teaching, and research in the campus community
	• Consults with the campus community to develop, implement, coordinate, and review initiatives/services/resources that support teaching, learning and research
	• Promotes the use of Library services and resources to the campus community, and as aligned to assigned subject areas or areas of expertise
	• Provides instruction in areas related to expertise

- Remains current and conversant with trends and practices within the Library and campus community by:
  - Maintaining general awareness of trends and developments in librarianship and academia
  - Maintaining awareness in areas of expertise and exploring potential local impacts or applications
  - Transferring knowledge to Library committees and staff, as well as faculty, staff and students, as appropriate
- Participates in, and at times leads, Library, University, and as appropriate, non-University committees and groups, and fosters collaboration, information sharing, partnerships and expertise as required
- Works with colleagues at other TUG, OCUL, CARL and ARL member institutions, as appropriate, in collaborative ventures
- Participates in professional development in areas such as research, courses, conference presentations, posters and ongoing skills acquisition

2. To ensure a thorough understanding of needs for information services and resources in the assigned subject areas and areas of expertise, the Liaison Librarian:

- Consults with Schools/Academic Departments to establish and prioritize their resources and services needs as well as to identify new opportunities for further collaboration
- Promotes the use of Library resources and services to Schools/Academic Departments
- Raises awareness of issues related to scholarly communication, including:
  - Maintaining general awareness of trends and development
  - Maintaining specific awareness in areas of expertise and exploring potential local impacts or applications
  - Transferring knowledge to School/Academic Department faculty, staff and students
- Provides curriculum specific library instruction to enhance the student experience
- Promotes lifelong learning
- Participates in the development and review of new and existing programs by working with the School/Academic Departments to:
  - Complete the Library portion of academic and accreditation program review reports, including new program reports. This includes participating in the initial review team meetings to gain a thorough understanding of the needs, learning outcomes, and career paths for graduating students and representing the Library during program review on-site visits
  - Review the curriculum, and seek meaningful opportunities to enhance student research skills, specialized information seeking, and critical analysis of information
  - Participate in curriculum reviews with particular regards to research skills, specialized information seeking, and critical analysis of information, as possible
- Remains well informed about the Library's resources, services and policies and interprets and promotes these to faculty and students
- Attends/participates in Faculty Council and Departmental meetings, as possible

3.	As a Liaison Librarian accountable for the proactive management of the collection lifecycle in assigned subject areas, the incumbent:
	• Develops and maintains collection development and retention policies that reflect the needs of Schools/Academic Departments and support long term management and relevance of the collection
	• Selects materials, both print and electronic, for the Library's collections in a fiscally responsible manner aiming to maximize the scope and depth of the collection
	• Analyzes the use of collections, and applies gained information to collection decisions
	• Evaluates the print and electronic collections and recommends actions based on condition and relevance of the collection
	• Collaborates with other Librarians and Library Department Heads regarding the selection and evaluation of interdisciplinary collections as well as the identification of locally unique, at times rare, collections

	• In co-operation with the Head, Collection Development and Heads, ISR, as appropriate:
	   o Interacts and negotiates with publishers/vendors
	   o Assesses vendors platforms & products and service
	   o Develops and maintains approval plan profiles
	   o Participates in the exploration and piloting of innovative collection development initiatives

	• Maintains current knowledge about the Acquisitions Budget and manages the budget allocations in a fiscally responsible manner, with particular attention to assigned Schools/Academic Departments
4.	As a Liaison Librarian providing support for information services and instructional activities, the incumbent:

	• Participates in Information Services delivery, including:
	   o Trains other Library staff for information service delivery, with particular regard to their assigned subject areas or areas of expertise
	   o Providing information services at virtual and/or physical service points
	   o Consultations to faculty and students, and staff

	• Participates in the Library's instructional activities, by:
	   o Developing, designing, delivering, and assessing instruction programs, including designing instructional materials, whether in person, online or in a blended environment
	   o Developing modules for instructional activities as related to areas of subject expertise
	   o Working with faculty to integrate the use of the collection, and research skills into course assignments and research activities

	• Designs, develops and maintains effective online and print content. Provides input to other Library departments into maintaining and improving the Library's virtual user interface and face to face services, including active participation in working groups
5.	As a Liaison Librarian who may be embedded in an academic School or Department that operates a Resource Centre, the incumbent:

	• Communicates with the Head, ISR (Davis or Porter) in regards to Resource Centre issues for discussion • Acts in an advisory capacity to Library and School on the functional operation of the Resource Centre, as appropriate. This excludes management of day-to-day responsibilities such as Circulation Services, Technical Services, troubleshooting equipment (printers, photocopiers, scanner, self-checkout unit), and management of employees • Advises on the implementation of Resource Centre policies to ensure that they are in keeping with Library and TUG-wide policies and practices • Participates with School/department staff in the coordination of activities for the delivery of information service • Oversees and makes decisions related to collection storage and maintenance • Communicates with School/department administration as appropriate
6.	As a Liaison Librarian who may undertake supervision of Library Associates and co-op students, the incumbent: • Coaches, trains and develops employee(s) to assure growth and development of that(those) individual(s) • Conducts regular performance reviews with direct report(s), and supports achievement of performance goals • Makes decisions on the hiring of his/her direct report(s), in consultation with the Head, ISR (Davis or Porter)

7.	As a Liaison Librarian and/or health information specialist who may have specialized areas of responsibility or expertise, the incumbent:
	
	• Actively participates on specialized teams or working groups to support the unique needs and strategic goals at the University of Waterloo. Activities could include for example:
	    ○ Participation in research projects and grant-funded projects as the information specialist
	    ○ Provision of training as related to areas of subject expertise
	• Ongoing, proactive acquisition, maintenance, and provision of leadership in the development of associated skills and knowledge in areas of expected expertise
	• Liaise, as Library representative, with campus partners such as the Writing Centre, Student Success Office on special projects beyond the scope of normal liaison activities with these partners

Position Requirements

Education:

ALA-accredited MLS/MLIS degree, or equivalent

Experience:

• Academic background and/or applicable knowledge of the specific liaison portfolio(s) demonstrated through undergraduate or advanced degree, coursework or work experience
• Proven excellent communication skills, both oral and written, and commitment to fostering positive working relationships & build partnerships
• Proven self-starter with demonstrated commitment to innovation, creativity, and

excellence
- Demonstrated ability to independently, as well as collaboratively, plan, coordinate, implement and assess effective services and collections projects, including managing multiple and simultaneous projects
- Demonstrated ability to analyze data and synthesize recommendations
- Proven ability to work effectively in a service oriented environment, which values collaboration and collegiality
- Demonstrated ability to interact with all staff in a respectful and sensitive manner

Technical:
- Knowledge of current practices and trends in the areas of interest to the specific liaison portfolio(s)
- Ability to develop, deliver and assess instructional content, in person and virtually, such as web content, screencasts, webinars
- Superior customer relationship management skills. Ability to maintain effective working relationships across multiple and diverse organizations, and across levels within organizations from specialist to executive level
- An understanding of the collection development process including principles of proactive information resources development and management, licensing and strong vendor relationships
- Excellent organizational, analytical and problem-solving skills
- Knowledge of current practices and trends in the areas of information services, information seeking, information literacy and instruction, information resources development and management, scholarly communication, and higher education
- Ability to identify new service and engagement opportunities, that align with Library and Campus Directions and to collaborate with library managers and colleagues on the feasibility, development and sustainability of new services and programs
- Ability and aptitude to use and learn new technologies to enhance and deliver information services
- Ability and aptitude to collaborate in an online, technology-rich environment
- Experience with financial and budget information
- Understands how research contributes to evidence-based decision-making

Assets:
- Experience in an academic Library setting
- Experience with information services delivery, in-person or virtual
- Experience providing instructional sessions, workshops, or presentations
- Demonstrated experience in leading and managing staff, including staff development and coaching

Technical:

MS Word	Excel	PowerPoint	Other
Intermediate	Intermediate	Intermediate	Intermediate web content development, Intermediate instructional methods and

technologies, Intermediate discovery and access interfaces

Nature and Scope

Interpersonal Skills:

Internally, communicates with employees in all groups and departments throughout the University community and at all levels to gather ideas, envision, articulate, update and inform on projects s/he is leading or otherwise accountable for. Externally, communicates frequently with vendors and colleagues at other institutions in order to execute work.

Level of Responsibility:

The position is responsible and accountable for the development and maintenance of high quality user-focused information resources and services, with particular focus on the assigned subject areas. The position is fully accountable for assigned Department/School acquisitions funds.

Decision-Making Authority:

Responsible and accountable for the development, delivery, and assessment of instructional services and collection decisions as related to assigned subject areas and/or project leadership. As required, the position consults with the Department Heads, ISR, and members of the Library Managers Group.

Physical and Sensory Demands:

Minimal exposure to disagreeable conditions typical of an office environment.

Working Environment:

Exposure to stresses related to pressures and priorities related to typical librarian responsibilities.

Has or develops expertise in a specialization that can be shared within and beyond the University of Waterloo

Human Resources
General Services Complex
University of Waterloo
200 University Avenue West
Waterloo, Ontario, Canada N2L 3G1
519 888 4567 ext. 35935

contact us | give us feedback | http://www.hr.uwaterloo.ca

MAKING THE **FUTURE**
SUPPORT WATERLOO

Responsibilities, Competencies, Goals

BRIGHAM YOUNG UNIVERISTY
HAROLD B. LEE LIBRARY
LIAISON LIBRARIAN PROFESSIONAL ASSIGNMENT EXPECTATIONS, PROFESSIONAL
DEVELOPMENT EXPECTATIONS, AND SCHOLARSHIP EXPECTATIONS

1. Librarianship: Professional Assignment

   a. Demonstrates effectiveness in serving as a liaison to faculty in assigned departments through:
      1) Reaching out to faculty
         a) Meeting and communicating regularly with the chair and teaching faculty in assigned academic departments
         b) Meeting all new faculty each year
         c) Coordinating with other librarians and curators regarding related/joint liaison assignments
      2) Developing collections and managing content in the assigned areas
         a) Developing and revising collection policy statements in assigned subjects
         b) Developing and managing print, electronic, and media collections in accordance with established policies and procedures in assigned subjects
         c) Evaluating collections regularly by conducting specific assessments with the purpose of identifying areas to improve or develop in support of faculty teaching and research
         d) Working with teaching faculty in assessing collections to support university curriculum
         e) Establishing, maintaining, and updating standing order and approval profiles with vendors
         f) Monitoring physical conditions of general collections, and making conservation and preservation decisions as needed
         g) Keeping students, teaching faculty, and library colleagues informed about new acquisitions
         h) Managing gift acquisitions for general collections in assigned subject areas
         i) Coordinating purchase of appropriate reference sources for the collection
      3) Promoting and providing Instruction in information literacy
         a) Analyzing curriculum of assigned departments, identifying and targeting critical courses (e.g. capstone courses, and other courses with a research component) for library instruction
         b) Developing and promoting instructional programs for undergraduates, graduates, and teaching faculty
         c) Teaching library instruction classes
         d) Providing individual library instruction in office
         e) Using assessment methods to evaluate student learning and improve instruction
         f) Promoting faculty and student understanding of contemporary scholarly communication issues and practices
         g) Marketing library resources and services in assigned areas

1

4) Providing reference/research support by
   a) Holding regular office hours for student and faculty consultations
   b) Answering phone, email, and other electronic inquiries from students, faculty, and the public
   c) Providing relevant online and print subject guides for faculty and students
   d) Maintaining a working knowledge of reference desk policy and procedures and training reference staff and student employees in specific tools and strategies in assigned subject areas
   e) Employing emerging technologies as appropriate
   f) Providing support for faculty in the areas of scholarly communications, including copyright, authors rights, data management, impact metrics and altmetrics
5) Promoting and coordinating of projects to digitize collections as appropriate,
   a) Acting as a consultant and content expert on digital projects related to assigned subject areas.
   b) Teaching courses in academic departments as requested and as appropriate

   2. Sets and accomplishes relevant goals within specified professional assignments.
b. Participates in committees that are a direct outgrowth of assigned professional responsibilities (See also 1.f.)
c. Achieves appropriate quantity and quality of work in assigned professional responsibilities.
d. Uses sound judgment in decision-making.
e. Manages personnel and resources effectively including submitting reports, keeping statistics, and managing appropriate budgets.

2. Librarianship: Professional Development

   a. Stays abreast of issues and trends in academic librarianship, higher education, and scholarly communication.
   b. Stays abreast of issues and trends in assigned subject areas.
   c. Stays abreast of scholarship in assigned subject areas, and other appropriate subject areas of expertise.
   d. Takes courses to enhance professional assignment and/or career opportunities.
   e. Studies professional literature.
   f. Attends conferences and workshops.
   g. Participates in appropriate professional associations.

3. Librarianship: Scholarship/Creative Work

   a. Collaborates with other faculty in appropriate research endeavours.
   b. Presents research or innovative/unique information in the assigned subject fields, and/or in the field of librarianship at conferences, workshops, seminars, and/or other professional meetings.
   c. Publishes significant and original contributions relevant to librarianship and/or to assigned subject areas.
   d. Curates exhibits that highlight unique library materials with a unified theme and context, providing significant educational opportunities for the campus community.
   e. Performs other approved scholarship/creative works.

2

UC, San Diego Academic Liaison Program

Description of Services

The ALP aims to integrate information services and competencies within academic programs in support of UC San Diego's teaching and research activities. We develop strategies to learn about and understand information needs of academic departments and programs; identify and implement effective methods to promote library services and resources; and provide subject-specific user services. Services include consultation by request; development and delivery of curriculum-related content; and instruction on library related topics identified through liaison relationships and user needs assessment, such as scholarly communications, publishing, research data management, copyright compliance and effective use of library resources. The ALP is also responsible for developing ways to effectively communicate academic research and teaching needs and priorities within the library, so that library policies, collections, and services are responsive to the interests and preferences of the academic community.

User Needs Research and Assessment

- Observational Methods
- Environmental scanning:

  Identify and describe research, educational and other campus user groups

  Track Research trends: topics, seminars, publications, Research Intelligence Portal, etc.

  Track curricula: faculty and staff continuing education; graduate and undergraduate curricular objectives. Identify and develop mapping tool in collaboration with learning services. Each program envisions using the tool for different projects with different mapping parameters.

  Attend or monitor campus public events, discussion forums, news streams.

  Document departmental and programmatic accreditation standards for library resources and services.

- Actively participate in the Library's external user advisory groups.
- Facilitate discipline-focused user advisory groups as needed, including faculty, staff and students.
- Investigational methods: Collaborate with other programs and Library Council to strategize and develop.
- Build and maintain a User Knowledge Base: User research and needs assessment will yield data to build and maintain a knowledge base of user needs that synthesizes observational data and enables the Library to respond to evolving demands. Such a knowledge base could be used to map UCSD library resources; services; outreach; information- and data literacy standards to campus programs, research and curricula.

The Liaison Program will provide leadership in communicating user priorities and preferences to The Library.

Communication, Outreach and Promotion

- Build an Outreach Toolkit: Core knowledge and about the Library and best practices for outreach.
- Develop and implement best practices for communications with users at a variety of levels.
- Construct systematic two-way communications channels
- Identify contact people for campus units, e.g. Head AAs, Dept network managers
- Develop and promote a program through which campus units will identify with specific liaisons
- Plan and deliver events targeted to specific, departmental user groups
- Informational: Talks, exhibits
- Promotional: participate in campus events to convey value, increase visibility, raise awareness
- Develop web presence
- Work with Digital User Services to determine how liaisons may best communicate through the Library website, e.g. deciding how and where to display Liaison contact page(s).
- Create specialized content for user web spaces.
- Orientation for new faculty, graduate students and staff (including research, administrative, and post-graduate staff)
- Create content for library communications as needed, e.g., campus newsletters, social networks, digital signage, etc.
- Provide office hours in user and library spaces

Research and Teaching Support

- Participate in Faculty Continuing Education: teach library-related topics identified through needs assessment or liaison relationships
- Provide consultation services for researchers
- We will document consultation topics and outcomes. Examples include effective use of library resources and services; scholarly publishing support; data management planning, and data curation support.
- Develop subject-specific instructional content and activities for faculty, staff, graduate, undergraduate education: workshops, guides, assignments, etc.
- Information Resource Support
- Identifying and linking appropriate resources to user sites
- Advising on appropriate use, citation, license restrictions
- Facilitating funding (e.g. Med Center, others?)
- Investigating user needs for collections and assisting in selection
- Assist departments and programs in ensuring that library-related accreditation standards are met.

Academic Partnerships: Building a Collaboration Framework

- Identify and expand upon best practices of existing liaison relationships
- Attend or participate in academic events and committees: e.g., research interest groups, research seminars, research or educational oversight, etc.
- Faculty Consultation: Specific needs expressed to liaison
- Participate in discipline-based professional organizations or conferences (Local, National, International)
- Network with information professionals from other institutions
- Learn current and emerging trends/priorities for discipline (publishing, teaching, research)
- Collaborate in mutually beneficial projects or events with users, e.g. publications, websites, presentations, etc.

Core Competencies: Department of Collections, Research, and Instruction
Last Revised July 8, 2014

Core Competencies Working Group
Jennifer Boettcher
Sandy Hussey
Judy McManus
Anna Simon
Melissa Van Vuuren

Table of Contents

Page | 1

Introduction

The following document outlines core competencies for the professional librarians in the Collections, Research, and Instruction Department (CRI) at Georgetown University. Its purpose is to define the competencies which delineate our professional roles and responsibilities in order for us to create accurate position descriptions, recruit competent librarians, provide uniform professional standards, and establish benchmarks for professional development. The competencies are grouped into the five accountabilities common to all CRI librarian position descriptions: liaison/outreach, instruction, reference, collection management, and professional development. The individual competencies tend to be conceptual in nature and are followed by "in practice" statements, which elucidate the ways in which each competency may be demonstrated.

While they identify commonalities amongst the CRI librarians, the core competencies are not intended to replace individual position descriptions. Rather, they are designed as a complementary document. Likewise the competencies are not evaluative in that they will not be used in the formal Annual Performance Review. They may, however, be used by individual librarians to identify potential annual goals. The competencies should encourage reflection and self-assessment leading to training, professional development, and excellence of service to the library and the university. Individuals are encouraged to develop their skills and knowledge beyond the core competencies.

These competencies were informed by current professional standards, guidelines, and competencies along with professional literature, which are available in Appendixes A and B.

The core competencies are a living document and will be reviewed every two years or as needed.

Page | 2

Liaison Core Competencies

Liaison work is the process by which librarians involve the library's clientele in the assessment, evaluation, and augmentation of collections and library services. It includes identifying user needs, evaluating and promoting existing collections and services, and locating resources that will enhance these offerings. Liaison work enables the library to communicate its collection policies and services to its clientele while enabling the constituency to communicate its needs and preferences to the library staff and governing body. Liaison work promotes the library's strategic goals and enhances its public relations.[1]

Core competency skills for liaison and outreach work were adopted and modified from Shreeves's "Iowa Framework for Liaisons/Subject Librarians."

Liaison Competency 1: Actively engages with faculty, students, and staff in assigned areas, developing strong working relationships.

In practice:
- Communicates on a regular basis with the appropriate constituencies for librarian's collection development areas.
- Communication can be directly with faculty, but also with student groups and support staff (such as the department administrator).
- Communication can take place via email, in-person, at department meetings, etc., and can be a combination of formal and informal.
- Communication should minimally include beginning of the semester introductions and end-of semester check-ins, as well as periodic promotion of services and collections (such as databases, website features, and acquisitions).

Liaison Competency 2: Promotes current services and collections.

In practice:
- Inform faculty, students, and appropriate staff when new resources are acquired or services are offered, asking for feed-back to improve services and collections.
- Under-utilized resources and services can also be promoted to increase visibility and use.
- Communicates library policies and procedures to faculty and students.
- Provides information on library initiatives such as data services, copyright, scholarly communication practices, and Digital Georgetown, as appropriate.

Liaison Competency 3: Analyzes trends in departmental teaching and research programs, stays abreast of scholarship in the disciplines themselves, and uses this knowledge to respond to departmental needs.

In practice:
- Works with appropriate department point people to monitor course offerings and department curricula, noting shifts in academic and pedagogic practices.

---

[1] Definition of liaison work adapted from RUSA

Page | 3

- Modifies library instruction, collection choices, and general liaison support to match the changing academic needs of the department, innovating new approaches as necessary.

Liaison Competency 4: Works closely with faculty and students to understand their changing workflows and patterns of scholarly communication.

In practice:

- By working closely with area faculty and students formally and informally via research consultations, library instruction, correspondence, attending department meetings and events as well as campus events, receiving department emails, etc., the liaison librarian monitors changing workflows and patterns of scholarly communication.

Liaison Competency 5: Seeks participation in academic departments.

In practice:

- The liaison librarian avails herself as a supportive member of the departments, as the situation allows.
- Asks to participate in or attend department meetings; attends annual department events, screenings, readings, presentations, colloquia, etc.
- Attends some larger campus events in which assigned departments may play a role.

Liaison Competency 6: Seeks opportunities to collaborate and establish partnerships with departments. Examples include:
  - o Collaboration with data producers and repository contributors.
  - o Partnering with researchers in projects, initiatives, and grants.

In practice:

- Considers where the department and the library's needs intersect within teaching, learning, and research initiatives and, when appropriate, seeks to support and align mutual goals.
- Supports teaching and learning initiatives such as ITEL, CNDLS's annual Teaching and Learning workshops, the new Writing and Culture Seminars, and SFS pro-seminar library instruction.
- In particular, participates in "trickle-down" initiatives, such as calls from the provost for the university to emphasize student research and writing opportunities as well as the use of primary sources within coursework, can contain opportunities for the library to repackage its services in a fresh and relevant fashion.

Liaison Competency 7: Supports the integration of information literacy skills into the curriculum.

In practice:

- Knows courses and curriculum in relevant subject departments and promotes, when appropriate, library instruction supporting general and subject-specific information literacy objectives.
- Develops awareness of common/current assignments in assigned areas.

Page | 4

Liaison Competency 8: Acquires functional knowledge of foreign languages, computer programs, academic resources, databases, and scholarly and research tools, as appropriate, that support the librarian's liaison responsibilities to the department.

In practice:
- Develops knowledge of foreign languages as necessary.
- In accordance with library policies, learns the appropriate level of software supporting specific and general research needs of academic programs such as digital scholarship, data, geospatial data and GIS, government information, streaming media programs, citation programs, visual resources, etc.
- In subject-specific instruction and consultations, is able to coach students, faculty, and staff on the use of this software, these academic resources, databases, and scholarly and research tools.

Page | 5

UIC Library Liaison Program: Activities, Competencies, and Indicators

The intention of the library liaison program is to provide faculty, staff, and students with a contact person in the library, who they can call upon for information about any library service, resource, or issue. Librarians are assigned to a department(s) on campus based on their education, experience, interests, and library needs. The liaison's primary role is to foster two-way communication between the library and the school. The liaison is expected to understand the information needs of his or her school as clearly as possible, and to represent those needs within the library. Liaisons are knowledgeable about library resources and services and will be able to represent these effectively to their contacts.

Activities of Library Liaisons

- Instruction:
    - Provide tailored workshops and general, course-specific or assignment specific instructional programs to meet specific needs
    - Offer demonstrations or workshops of resources and services of interest to departments
    - Map information literacy to college/ departmental competencies
    - Learn about college/ department instruction and research focus
        - Meet with department chair or other leaders to learn about directions of department/ college, seek feedback on library services and collections
        - Attend department/ group meetings or other functions
        - Review departments/ colleges website and strategic goals
        - Periodic searches for faculty publications output
        - Participate in professional development activities to enhance skills and knowledge to support assigned college or department
    - Develop and maintain necessary subject and class-specific LibGuides
    - Document activities related to curriculum integrated instruction (contact names of instructors, documentation of instruction outline) so that transitions of liaisons allow as much continuity as possible
    - ALA Professional Standards for Proficiencies for Instruction Librarians and Coordinators: http://www.ala.org/acrl/standards/profstandards
- Communicate with college / department about new resources, changes in resource functionality/features, and cancellations
    - Prepare and distribute targeted library information news updates
    - Send out annual Liaison letter and send to targeted audience as appropriate/ possible
    - 100 ways to Reach Your Faculty
- New faculty
    - Send information packets for new faculty
    - Provide one-on-one orientation to new faculty members and teaching assistants
- Provide one-on-one reference and consultations to faculty, staff, and students on database searches – provide tailored database instruction or assist with developing search strategy through email, in-person, and online
- Collections development

- o Develop and manage relevant print and online collections
- o Review database and journal subscriptions each year, and consider cancellation of those with little use in order to free up funds for new needed resources.
- o Determine which resources are being used in the curriculum or by students, as that may impact retention decisions.
- o Respond to faculty and student resource requests
- o Determine the needs and priorities of users
- o Monitor new resources in your areas for collection consideration and assess potential new resources when available for trial
- o Seek feedback when making decisions in updating the library's collections
- o Gather information about department's/ college's research needs and how the library's collections can support them
- o Monitor budget and participate in cost reduction/cancellation projects as needed
- o Withdraw duplicates and material that is no longer current or out of scope as appropriate for the college or department and Library collections policies of the particular UIC Library
- o Make decisions about donations in consultation with Collections Coordinator and RAM at Daley, Health Sciences Bibliographer at LHS. Regions would consult with Health Sciences Bibliographer when needed.
- Additional activities
  - o Schedule office hours in college/ department/ labs
  - o Write a feature or column for departmental newsletters
  - o Attend morning report or department rounds (as appropriate)
  - o Provide mediated searches on clinical queries (as appropriate)
  - o Assist with college re-accreditation

Competencies of Library Liaisons

- Be able to articulate curricular and research developments in college/ department
- Design and present instruction in person or through online tutorials or other learning objects
- Information Resources
  - o Be able to describe and demonstrate proficiency in searching the key databases/ clinical tools in your liaison role and the other disciplines supported by your UIC library
  - o Be able to demonstrate proficiently how to search key databases/ clinical tools in liaison role and in key databases used by other disciplines supported by your UIC library
  - o Direct patrons to appropriate databases for information needs
  - o Search using strategies to retrieve relevant articles
- Provide basic support of citation management tools such as RefWorks and be able to refer advanced questions to appropriate library faculty
- Critically appraise and assess the evidence/ literature retrieved

2 | UIC Library Liaison Activities, Competencies, and Indicators, July 2015

Collections Development

o Develop the collections and make informed subject collection decisions based on faculty and student needs; conduct use assessments of electronic and print resources for retention/cancellation decisions.
o Know the content of each resource in your area and understand the overlap with other resources. The content will affect the types of usage statistics received and what they mean.
o Know what are the core resource(s) and journals for your subject areas, the ones that are critical to support the program.
o Understand the resource acquisition process.
  o Be able to explain the difference between a journal in a full-text EBSCO database and a journal subscription from EBSCO, and what the long-term archival rights are for each.
  o Understand what a journal embargo is and how it affects patrons, and what are the options in case of an embargo.
  o Understand and be able to "read" the Voyager Budget Reports and the Detailed Fund Report (DFR)
  o Be aware of what journals relevant to your subject areas are in the current Big Deals.
  o Be able to look up basic e-resource data in Serials Solutions
  o Be able to login and utilize the CARLI selection system, EBSCOnet, and GOBI.
o Know how to collect or obtain use statistics for your resources in order to evaluate use.
  o Understand what use statistics definitions mean, and the difference between COUNTER-compliant and non-compliant statistics, and the differences between vendor and Serials Solutions statistics.
o Understand why some journals may have use statistics from multiple sources and what the differences are.

Data Management

o Provide basic guidance in data management strategies
  o Librarians can assist patrons in locating existing data repositories and data sets
  o Librarians can assist researchers in identifying storage options for data -- either subject repositories or a campus repository; appropriately know when to refer to INDIGO/local repository vs other repositories
  o Librarians are aware of special requirements for data in specific domains / disciplines (e.g. Medical--HIPAA; personally identifiable data in social science research, etc.)
  o Librarians can assist researchers in identifying federal, grant, or journal mandates for data access and restrictions
  o Librarians are knowledgeable of the data lifecycle process for research and can provide direction for each stage to research faculty
  o Librarians are aware of services provided by and the experts within the library and make an appropriate referral

- o Librarians can refer patrons to the DMPTool
- o Librarians can explain how to cite data in articles
- o Librarians can communicate/advocate/ market the library's role in data management to users
- o See <u>Liaison Librarian Competencies</u>

Scholarly Communications

- o Liaisons are able to articulate issues in scholarly communication and describe scholarly communication/ open access/ publishing services offered by library
- o Liaisons are knowledgeable about and are able to speak to a range of scholarly communication issues, including rising journals costs, new models for publishing, publishing fees, open access memberships, relevant legislation, UIC initiatives, author rights, open access.
  - ▪ Help faculty and graduate students to understand their rights as authors
  - ▪ Promote use of CIC addendum
  - ▪ Promote use of Creative Commons License
  - ▪ Advocate for sustainable models of scholarly communication
- o Support and promote Library SC initiatives (INDIGO@UIC, Journals@UIC, open access memberships)
  - ▪ INDIGO@UIC
    - • Helping administrators, faculty, and students understand the role of the INDIGO in preserving and promoting scholarship
    - • Assist in content recruitment; identify content appropriate for IR
  - ▪ Journals@UIC
    - • Promote Journals@UIC as an alternative to traditional publishers for publishing journals
  - ▪ ROAAP Fund
  - ▪ Promote UIC Research Open Access Article Publishing (ROAAP) Fund
  - • See <u>Scholarly Communication Competencies for UIC Librarians</u>

Special Collections & Archives

- o Level one (all liaisons)
  - o Have a general understanding of SCUA unit organization and know the SCUA liaisons within the department: Val Harris, rare books, Peggy Glowacki, manuscripts; Megan Keller, Chicago Mercantile Exchange; Kevin O'Brien, Health Sciences
  - o Refer inquiries to appropriate staff, usually via QP or the LibChat IM queue.
  - o Have a general knowledge of SCUA policies and procedures, including public hours, how researchers access collections.
- o Level two (liaisons with relevant disciplines):
  - o Have reviewed SCUA holdings for their subject area in person.
  - o Be able to describe, in general, SCUA holdings relevant to their subject area (e.g., for sociology, we hold papers of a number of cultural organizations and social service agencies particularly related to Eastern European immigration

in the late nineteenth and early twentieth century; for health sciences, we hold rare and historical works on women's health, particularly pregnancy, childbirth, surgery, and fertility).
- o Be able to explain use of SCUA discovery tools such as finding aids to instructional faculty and students.
- o Incorporate discussion of SCUA as part of bibliographic instruction on primary source research.

Government Information

- o **Government structures/levels, processes and administrative structures and their profound influence on the bibliographic control of government information.** Government information is often based on long-term programs over several decades and different political elections. Much of this depends on earlier decisions or analysis that may or may not be directly mentioned or referred to. Very often several/many years of these types of documents have to be found or read for the user to understand the context of the question or government information that they seek.
- o **Understanding legislation, regulations, legal decisions, and public statements.** Understand, and be able to explain to the user, how the basic laws are created, implemented and adjudicated and how this process determines where the information can be found.
- o **Government data sources and reports.** Government data can be raw, analyzed to a limited degree or fully explained. There is no single place to look for government data or reports. However, there are several critical web pages and data depository sites one can consult.
- o **Understand the "gray literature": a shared information world between public and private organizations.** Over the last 35 years, non-government special interest groups, political parties, professional associations, and other non-government organizations have produced or co-created government information. They may not necessarily be issued by a government agency, but they are often distributed through government information programs.
- o **Understand when to use "digital" government information and services.** For the last ten years, many e-government processes and services are integrating more public information sources with deeply complicated government processes and services directed at the individual citizen. This includes regulatory, financial, statistical and environmental information. Very often these information sources are only available through stand-alone databases, or digital record keeping, managed by a particular government agency or contractor.
- o **Understand the history and organization of government information collections at UIC:**
  The Paper Universe
  The Gray Literature Universe
  The Digital Universe
- o **Learn how to answer reference questions with possible government information resources.**

Potential Indicators of Success / Integration of Library Liaisons

Note: Not all indicators are appropriate for all liaisons. Accomplishing items on the list are potential indicators of successful integration / communication with a college/ department.

- Collaboration in conducting a narrative or systematic literature searching with appropriate co-author designation as appropriate
- Teach a course or course component
- Establish a teaching partnership with faculty in college
- Increase teaching partnerships
- Attend departmental events and meetings, faculty meetings, or lab meetings on a regular basis
- Participate in departmental events and meetings – present on databases, service, or topic
- Serve on departmental task force, committee, or council
- Serve on departmental curriculum committees
- Establish a research partnership with faculty in college
- Develop a program that promotes active student-centered learning
- Liaison is known by assigned college's faculty
- Receive faculty status within the college or department
- Included on departmental or college listservs

OVERVIEW

Academic Liaisons support faculty and students by engaging with them throughout the research teaching, and learning processes. Each liaison has assigned subject and/or functional areas and actively participates in the common responsibilities outlined below.

Each liaison also serves on one of the following teams:

- **Collections:** work collaboratively with the Collections Analyst to develop and assess collections guided by a deep understanding of the research trends and local needs;
- **Teaching and Learning:** actively engage with faculty and graduate students as partners in programmatically integrating information fluency concepts and research skills into the curriculum;
- **Marketing and Services:** work collaboratively with the UX Director and colleagues in Access Services and Support Services using user-centered inquiry and design to develop, market, assess, and maintain relevant, high-quality services;
- **Scholarly Communications:** work collaboratively with the UX Director to understand faculty and students changing workflows and patterns of scholarly communication and assist in the development of tools and services to support this work.

COMMON RESPONSIBILITIES

Liaison Engagement
- Actively engage with faculty and students to build strong working relationships
- Be knowledgeable about and be able to speak to a range of library issues, including scholarly communication, data management and curation, digital scholarship, and information fluency
- Identify opportunities to collaborate on projects, exhibits, services, and collection decisions
- Actively seek opportunities to support constituents through all parts of the research lifecycle
- Analyze trends in departmental teaching and research programs, stay abreast of scholarship in assigned disciplines, and use this knowledge to respond to departmental needs

Content (Acquisition, Stewardship and Promotion)
- Monitor and analyze faculty and graduate student research trends in assigned areas
- Understand the broader research and scholarly communication trends in assigned areas and their relationship to the local environment
- Develop, discover and recruit institutional scholarly output, such as research data, digital content, and other content for inclusion in digital repositories
- Understand collection policies and budgets as a part of overall planning
- Develop research level collections by curating the acquisition of materials in all formats that support the research and teaching not only of the assigned departments but also of those interdisciplinary areas which build from them.
- Evaluate and make decisions about existing collections including decisions about withdrawal, transfer, and preservation
- Promote newly acquired and accessioned materials through integration into instruction, class syllabi and exhibits

- Instruct on, and troubleshoot, electronic resources
- Work closely and proactively with the Collections Group

Teaching and Learning
- Stay current with relevant University and/or department curriculum initiatives; communicate new directions to the Teaching and Learning group
- Demonstrate core pedagogical competencies in assigned instruction areas, including the methods of disciplinary instruction in those areas
- Work closely and proactively with the Teaching and Learning Group
- Determine the most effective way to incorporate information fluency into formal and informal instructional settings

Research Support
- Customized and expert:
  - Provide consultations that involve subject or other specialized areas of expertise (e.g. in-depth knowledge of specific collection or specific scholarly communication issues)
  - Apply knowledge of how research is conducted in assigned disciplines
  - Record consultations and regularly analyze them to discern trends in research areas

- On-demand
  - Provide professional, high-quality research support to faculty and students who use our on-demand resources, including staffing the Research Consultation Office, being on call, and monitoring e-mail and chat reference

Scholarly Communication
- Be knowledgeable about and able to communicate with faculty and students on the range of scholarly communication issues, including open access, copyright, authors' rights, and metrics.
- Collaborate with DMS to connect researchers to data management resources
- Collaborate with the IR unit to provide education about the services they provide
- Assist faculty and graduate students with the identification of themselves as unique authors, the association of themselves with their body of work, and the dissemination of that body of work

QUALIFICATIONS:
- MLS from an ALA-accredited institution or related graduate degree with a minimum of three years professional experience in library research, instruction and collection development
- Strong technology skills including experience with innovative applications of instructional and communication technologies, wikis, (i.e. Confluence or a similar platform), AdobeConnect, screen capture software and LibGuides
- Demonstrated academic liaison experience
- Demonstrated commitment to responsive and quality library services
- Strong teaching, interpersonal, and communication skills, including demonstrated ability to work collaboratively
- Willingness to work a flexible schedule, including occasional evenings and weekends

PREFERRED QUALIFICATIONS:
- Advanced degree in the humanities, sciences, social sciences, or engineering
- Experience working in an academic or research library

ACADEMIC LIAISON AND SELECTOR JOB ADDENDUM

Academic liaison and selector assignments entail responsibilities related to faculty outreach, reference and instruction, collections, and other services as outlined below.

This document describes the responsibilities of liaisons and selectors. For individuals whose job descriptions do not already include such a description, this wording can be appended to establish a record of understanding between supervisor and supervisee with regard to liaison and/or selection assignments. The addendum provides a set of guidelines for liaisons and selectors to follow throughout the year.

LIAISON ASSIGNMENTS: The following responsibilities will fall to librarians with liaison assignments, whether or not they also have selection assignments:

1. Establish and maintain regular contact with faculty and students in assigned academic units or other non-academic constituency groups, serving as a link between the user community and the library.

2. Develop and maintain awareness of programs and courses, faculty research and curriculum support needs; evaluate library services and resources required to meet university teaching, learning, and research needs of assigned constituency.

3. Actively assist users in assigned constituencies locate and use information resources, directing them to appropriate librarians, collections, and services within and outside NU.

4. Provide or facilitate research consultations and instruction to faculty and students in assigned constituency groups.

5. Contribute to the library's outreach program through participation in disciplinary clusters; attend faculty or other departmental meetings whenever possible.

6. Address scholarly communication matters and direct faculty to appropriate resources relevant to open access, copyright, new publishing models, pricing, and related issues.

7. Promote library collections and services both on and off campus; design and maintain research guides(s) to support assigned constituency groups.

8. Help ensure that collections in all formats are responsive to constituent group needs by acting as a selector (see below), by communicating and collaborating with (other) selectors with relevant assignments, and by suggesting purchases for specialized resources.

SELECTION ASSIGNMENTS: The following responsibilities will fall to librarians with selection assignments, whether or not they have liaison assignments:

Liaison/Selector Addendum | Page 1

OHIO UNIVERSITY LIBRARIES
SUBJECT LIBRARIANS FRAMEWORK

*Subject librarians actively engage with faculty, students, and staff in assigned departments in order to develop strong, collaborative, opportunistic relationships that **place the Libraries in the flow of teaching, learning, and research.***

Subject librarians use their knowledge and expertise in these activities:

- Collection Development & Management - Identifying, developing, and promoting collections that support research and curricular needs
- Teaching & Learning - designing and implementing strategic and pedagogically appropriate instruction, reference and research consultation services using a variety of methods
- Scholarly Communication - educating and informing faculty, graduate students and campus administrators on issues of scholarly communication
- Data Management – educating and informing researchers on issues of data architectures, policies, practices and procedures that properly manage the full lifecycle needs of research data.
- Fundraising & Grant Writing - participating in development and fundraising efforts and cultivating relationships with established and potential donors as appropriate; identifying potential projects and activities for grant funding; seeking opportunities to support and collaborate on grant funded projects of the departments
- Special/Digital Collections – identifying and fostering connections between the curriculum and research and the Libraries' special collections

In order to be successful in the above activities, librarians must:

- Understand the curriculum of the department and identify and promote appropriate integration of library collections and services into that curriculum
- Be aware of and monitor changes in the research areas of departmental faculty
- Understand user needs and information-seeking behaviors
- Facilitate ongoing communication about resource needs and service expectations
- Understand basic pedagogical methods and information literacy theory
- Understand and speak knowledgeably about national trends within the discipline on issues of scholarly communication and data management
- Share information about users with library staff and with departments
- Use assessment, data analysis and evaluation to improve and prioritize

Ohio State University Libraries
Research & Education Division
Librarian Position Description Framework

Introduction to the Framework

This document describes a spectrum of activities and is intended to support development and revision of position descriptions for librarians in the Research and Education division. Clear and current position descriptions, along with department/division goals and the Libraries strategic plan, will help individuals write annual personal goals.

The R&E Framework describes most work performed by public service librarians and is based on the framework developed by the University of Minnesota Libraries and the core competencies identified in the Libraries' Engaged Librarian Framework:
http://library.osu.edu/staff/administration-reports/Engaged_Librarian_Framework_Dec2011.pdf

Specific additional competencies for functional specialist positions (e.g. instruction, assessment, etc.) are not addressed here and will be identified by department heads as they write or revise position descriptions. This framework also does not specify expectations for research and service activities that may be included in full position descriptions for Libraries faculty.

Liaison

- ☐ Actively engage and communicate effectively with faculty, students, and staff in assigned areas, developing strong working relationships.
- ☐ Seek opportunities to collaborate and establish partnerships with departments, including the creation of digital content, strategies for managing data and information, and support for researchers in projects or grants that require intense information and data management.
- ☐ Promote current services and collections.
- ☐ Be knowledgeable about and be able speak to a range of library issues, including scholarly communication, digital initiatives, the development of new online tools, and the integration of information literacy skills into the curriculum.
- ☐ Assess user needs to develop and maintain relevant, high-quality services and collections.
- ☐ Analyze trends in departmental teaching and research programs, stay abreast of scholarship in the disciplines themselves, and use this knowledge to respond to departmental needs.
- ☐ Champion the library as an intellectual meeting place for programming, conversation, and inquiry.

Research Services

- ☐ Analyze and understand users' research and information needs to develop, refine, assess, and sustain research and information services and programs in all formats.
- ☐ Actively seek opportunities to foster interdisciplinary collaborations in the provision of research and information services across the campus.
- ☐ Provide research consultations that involve subject or other specialized areas of expertise (e.g., in-depth knowledge of copyright or scholarly communication issues or specific collections).

DRAFT, 8/6/2015

☐ Provide on-demand research and information support in multiple formats.
☐ Continuously evaluate and assess research and information-related services.

Scholarly Communication

☐ Understand the scholarly communication process, publishing models, and emerging trends in assigned disciplines.
☐ Educate and inform faculty, graduate students, and campus administrators about scholarly communication issues and Libraries programs and services in this area.
☐ Understand and explain the principles behind open access publishing, institutional repositories, and authors' rights.
☐ Promote OSU Libraries publishing partnership options.
☐ Advocate for sustainable models of scholarly communication.

Collection Development and Management

☐ Systematically select material in all formats to serve the current and future research, teaching, and learning needs of clientele in the subject areas of XXX.
☐ Build on collections of distinction that may also serve regional, national and international users.
☐ Discover and recruit institutional scholarly output, research data and other content for inclusion in the University Libraries' digital initiatives.
☐ Develop cooperative statewide collection development relationships to enhance collaboration, access, and the development of shared resources.
☐ Manage collection funds efficiently, effectively and in a timely manner.
☐ Strategically assess and make decisions regarding the acquisition, retention and preservation of collections.
☐ Work effectively with colleagues in the Libraries to enhance acquisition, access, discovery, and use of library collections.

Teaching and Learning

☐ Actively engage with faculty and graduate teaching assistants as partners in programmatically integrating information literacy concepts and skills into the curriculum.
☐ Maintain an up-to-date knowledge of relevant University and department curriculum initiatives, in order to keep the information literacy program consistent with University curriculum.
☐ Identify areas where new online learning and digital tools can place the Libraries into the flow of teaching, learning and research.
☐ Collaborate in the design, implementation, and maintenance of online tools and services that meet the needs of discipline/interdisciplinary research communities.
☐ Understand and apply basic principles of instructional and assignment design, develop effective instructional materials and sessions in a variety of formats and provide alternative learning opportunities.
☐ Conduct needs assessment as appropriate to plan new areas of instructional initiative and selectively measure instructional outcomes in order to ensure effectiveness of instructional programs.
☐ Engage in reflective teaching through the use of instructional improvement tools available from the Libraries' Teaching & Learning Office and the university.

DRAFT, 8/6/2015

Fund Raising

- ☐ Identify and monitor relevant government agencies and private foundations for funding opportunities.
- ☐ Identify potential projects / activities for grant funds; prepare and submit grant proposals.
- ☐ Identify potential donors and work with the Libraries Development Office to cultivate donors as appropriate.
- ☐ Seek input from academic department heads and faculty about needs that might be met with external funding.

Management and Supervision

- ☐ Coordinate overall operational activities of [name of unit or library]; facilitating relationships with other groups in the Libraries, evaluating needs and processes, addressing staffing requirements, physical plant needs, and the implementation of policies and procedures.
- ☐ Provide direct supervision of [positions]. In consultation with department director write position descriptions, hire, assign job responsibilities, coach and mentor, conduct performance evaluations, and facilitate staff development and training opportunities.
- ☐ Prepare narrative and statistical reports for [name of unit or library] and prepare additional documentation on activities and progress as required. Prepare recommendations and proposals for long range projections in terms of staffing, space and equipment, and collection facility needs.

DRAFT, 8/6/2015

 UNIVERSITY LIBRARIES

A Framework for the Engaged Librarian: Building on our Strengths

The role of subject librarians in academic libraries continues to evolve because of the changes occurring throughout higher education—changes marked by simultaneous hyperspecialization and interdisciplinarity, by the movement of learning experiences toward the online and the mobile, and by changes in user behaviors in library spaces, where traditional reference service is less needed in a time of ubiquitous access to information resources, but where greater explanation, context-setting, and interpretation is needed for many library users to make sense of their research projects within a rapidly changing environment, and where positioning subject librarian expertise within the workflows of users is crucial.

To respond to this environment, The Ohio State University Libraries have made "engagement" a priority for subject librarians, and Area Studies and Special Collections Librarians. The kind of deepened involvement with the academic community envisioned by "engagement" calls for a new Framework, which presents an organized approach to professional activity with "engagement" as the linchpin or guiding principle.

How the Framework will be Used

The Framework for the Engaged Librarian presented here draws on the best thinking of the Engaged Librarian Framework Group in the OSU Libraries, and on the documents on subject librarians and engaged librarianship developed first by the University of Minnesota Libraries (Librarian Position Description Framework); the University of Iowa Libraries (Iowa Framework for Liaisons/Subject Librarians) and Duke University Libraries (Engaging with Library Users: Sharpening Our Vision as Subject Librarians for the Duke University Libraries).

This Framework presents the main categories of engaged librarian responsibilities, and serves to create expectations for all subject librarians at OSUL (including Area Studies and Special Collections Librarians). The Framework will be used

to set goals each year for all subject librarians. Each of the five sections in the Framework contains a list of competencies. All competencies should be considered "core" for all subject librarians, but will be considered developmental as the Engaged Librarian Model is implemented over time. In addition, each section has a list of "best practices" enumerating sample activities, projects, or behaviors that illustrate engagement . Subject librarians, in consultation with their division heads and supervisors, will develop their list of goals each year, using the competencies identified, and the best practices examples as a guide. Their goals will also be based on disciplinary distinctions and other aspects of their assignments.

Engagement

Engagement is a deepened level of sustained, high-quality, mutually beneficial interaction in the liaison role with academic programs.

Competencies:

• Communicating effectively with members of the assigned departments, individually or in groups, in both face-to-face and virtual venues

• Developing partnerships when appropriate between the library and the assigned area on collection building, teaching and learning issues, grants or research projects, or other areas of mutual interest

• Creating new programs and services (or improving existing programs and services) that respond to identified needs and priorities of students and faculty and to strategic directions of the Library

• Facilitating problem-solving for the assigned programs in relation to library services

• Championing the library as an intellectual meeting place for programming, conversation, and inquiry

Examples of best practices:

• Communicating often with faculty, students, academic staff, and administrators in assigned areas

• Participating in departmental meetings and other events such as colloquia, seminars or dissertation defenses

• Participating in discipline-specific organizations and associations

• Inviting faculty to share their scholarship through library-sponsored programs and events

Research Services

Provide expert research consultation to members of the university community through understanding user needs, extending specialized services to users appropriate for their discipline and points in their research workflow, and assessing the services offered in order to improve them.

Competencies:

• Analyzing and understanding users' research and information needs to develop, refine, assess, and sustain research and information services and programs in all formats

• Actively seeking opportunities to foster interdisciplinary collaborations in the provision of research and information services across the campus

• Providing research consultations that involve subject or other in-depth specialized areas of expertise

• Providing on-demand research and information support in multiple formats

• Continuously evaluating and assessing research and information-related services

Examples of best practices:

• Developing and conducting studies to assess users' research, information, and technology needs (using data from Ask Database, web logs, circulation statistics, ILL Statistics, interviewing key constituents)

• Sharing information with colleagues about disciplinary trends and OSUL/University activities

• Creating research portals, research wikis, research blogs, and other virtual tools and resources

• Offering regular virtual and in-person office hours in departments

• Creating and maintaining appropriate online research guides, tutorials, etc.

• Regularly surveying departmental web sites, listservs, press releases, OSUToday, onCampus and other appropriates sources to identify faculty research interests, announcements of new University initiatives and centers, etc.

• Contributing to Subject Teams and other groups in planning services for interdisciplinary projects and strategic priorities at the campus level

• Establishing research mentorships with students writing undergraduate theses

The Ohio State University Libraries

Scholarly Communication

Work with members of the university community to enhance their ability to share their research broadly and effectively by addressing a range of issues, including changes in publishing, funder requirements for sharing research, open access models for disseminating new knowledge, digital publishing, and exercising author rights to broaden sharing of research.

Competencies:

• Knowing how scholarly communication works (including understanding a variety of publishing models) in assigned disciplines

• Tracking emerging trends and models within disciplines and how these relate to trends in other disciplines

• Understanding and explaining the value and function of OSUL publishing partnership options as they develop

• Explaining the principles behind open access publishing and public access practices, knowing expectations of funders for sharing research results, and knowing available options for open access for scholars in their assigned departments

• Understanding and explaining the functions and policies of institutional repositories and disciplinary repositories generally and OSU-supported repositories specifically.

• Understanding the mechanics of authors' copyrights and advise faculty and students on strategies for effectively managing and exercising their rights in their works.

Examples of best practices:

• Helping faculty, graduate students, and academic staff to negotiate retaining their rights as authors to broaden access to their research.

• Advocating with authors and editors for advancing sustainable models of scholarly communication.

• Providing resources that increase faculty, graduate students, and academic staff awareness of alternative publication models in their discipline.

• Working with faculty to deposit their works in institutional or disciplinary repositories and publish in open access venues.

• Recruiting university-published content; identifying digital resources that require long-term preservation and merit sustained access.

• Referring faculty, students, and staff to the Head of the Copyright Resources Center, Preservation and Reformatting Officer, or the Scholarly Resources Integration Department when appropriate and partnering with them in projects that increase sharing of OSU research.

Collection Development

Develop and manage collections to actively support research and instruction in subject area(s) by contributing to the selection and management of content for the libraries collections in relevant formats and languages.

Competencies:

• Using collections as a basis for engagement to create dynamic services and innovative applications of collections to research questions or curricular goals

• Managing funds and other resources to support the acquisition of content that has the most value for OSU research, teaching, and learning.

• Working effectively with colleagues in the Libraries to enhance acquisition, access, discovery, and use of library collections.

• Integrating knowledge of scholarly communication patterns and trends in a discipline with local collection building and management activities.

• Developing cooperative statewide collection development relationships to enhance collaboration, access and the development of shared resources

• Developing and applying knowledge of local use of collections to effectively manage resources and increase the value of collections for users' research, teaching, and learning.

Continued

The Ohio State University Libraries

Collection Development
continued

Examples of best practices:

• Applying knowledge of changing user needs and behaviors to review continuing commitments and approval plans regularly to ensure our collections reflect current research and scholarship on campus;

• Expending collection funds effectively and in a timely manner;

• Identifying new content (e.g. e-resources) that advances research or teaching at OSU and creatively seeking resources to acquire it.

• Participating actively in managing print retention and maintaining print collections within shelf capacity

• Analyzing usage data for electronic or print collections and revising purchase recommendations in response.

• Developing and maintaining relationships with donors (both in-kind and monetary) and dealers.

Engaged Librarian Framework Working Group

Tschera Connell
Tamar Chute
Florian Diekmann
Maureen Donovan
Anne Fields
Kathy Webb
Craig Gibson

Teaching and Learning

Collaborate with colleagues within and beyond the libraries on planning, delivering, improving, and assessing information literacy initiatives within the context of the larger curriculum of the university.

Competencies:

• Promoting understanding among faculty and other teaching staff about approaches to integrating information literacy concepts and skills into the curriculum

• Understanding basic principles of instructional and assignment design appropriate to information literacy instruction

• Using program assessment data to plan new areas of instructional initiative

• Developing effective instructional sessions and provide alternative learning opportunities (research consultations, Carmen Library Links, etc.)

• Engaging in reflective teaching through the use of instructional improvement tools that are available from UCAT (University Center for the Advancement of Teaching) and the Library's Teaching and Learning Office

• Understanding basic copyright principles and recognize basic areas of application (e.g. fair use scenarios and face-to-face teaching exceptions)

Examples of best practices:

• Analyzing curriculum within assigned subject areas and prepare curriculum maps or other curriculum plans for information literacy competencies

• Negotiating with teaching faculty on timing, purpose, and learning outcomes for information literacy instruction

• Writing learning outcomes for information literacy appropriate to their disciplines

• Using appropriate assessment techniques to gather and analyze information on student learning and information needs in preparing instruction

• Developing learning materials in a variety of formats for a variety of teaching situations (e.g., materials for faculty or GTAs to use for class sessions)

• Teaching classes effectively using a variety of pedagogies

• Creating learning environments using appropriate e-learning technologies or systems

• Working with staff in the Libraries' Teaching and Learning Office in improving instruction and to incorporate new technologies and effective e-learning strategies

• Performing regular teaching self-assessments

The Ohio State University Libraries

The UNIVERSITY of OKLAHOMA LIBRARIES libraries.ou.edu	University Libraries **POSITION DESCRIPTION FRAMEWORK FOR LIAISON LIBRARIANS**

The University of Oklahoma Libraries represent a strategic investment of the university that is essential to support of the teaching, research, and service missions of the University.

Liaison librarians serve as the primary contact between the University Libraries and academic departments, schools, colleges, and/or programs or centers. The nature of the liaison role requires librarians to develop and maintain positive working relationships with faculty, students, staff, and scholars and other campus constituencies in ways that enhance the strategic investment of OU in libraries as part of the research and educational infrastructure of the institution. The primary focus of a liaison's role is to build and sustain relationships.

Liaison librarians work to enhance the visibility of library services across the campus and seek input and feedback from faculty, students, staff, and scholars about library services and programs in ways that ensure the libraries meet the current and emerging needs of the institution and are able to provide sustainable and scalable services.

Liaison librarians act as expert guides to the research and scholarly literature of specific disciplines; provide research support and consultation at the point of need; teach classes and workshops on research tools, methods and strategies; curate research-level collections that include both print and electronic materials as well as special collections; and support development of emerging forms of digital scholarship.

In order to actively promote research and educational services and facilitate research and scholarship within the evolving scholarly communication ecosystem and higher education environment of research universities, liaisons are expected to be proactive in developing and maintaining their professional expertise and knowledge of current and emerging changes, trends, and issues in the rapidly changing environments of academic librarianship and specific disciplines.

****

Liaison duties fall into the teaching category for library faculty, a category that generally covers between 60 to 80 percent of a library faculty member's time. Liaison duties are part of the primary job responsibilities for a professional librarian.

The specific duties of a liaison librarian fall into several areas and generally include the following specific duties:

1. Serves as the liaison librarian for the following assigned areas: _____.
2. Serves as an embedded librarian, physically located within the _____ either full- or part-time. Provides personalized consultation services to faculty and students within the department/college/school. Offers library services and programs custom designed for constituency. [APPLICABLE ONLY TO LIBRARIANS EMBEDDED INTO SPECIFIC DEPARTMENTS/COLLEGES/SCHOOLS]

RELATIONSHIP DEVELOPMENT

3. Develops and maintains positive working relationships outside the library with administrators, library representatives, faculty, and students in academic and affiliated units for assigned subject areas. Meets and/or communicates regularly with administrators and library representatives.

Page 1 of 3

4. Communicates regularly with department faculty and students through email, LISTSERVs, departmental websites or other channels as appropriate. Attends departmental meetings of academic departments, schools, and colleges and/or holds regular office hours in academic departments, schools, and colleges if applicable.
5. Establishes and sustains positive working relationships with all levels of staff – administrators, faculty, staff, and student employees – within the library.

SCHOLARLY COMMUNICATION

6. Develops and maintains working knowledge of scholarly communication and open access developments and trends as well as local, statewide, regional, and national initiatives in order to be able to consult with faculty and students and provide support for campus-level initiatives.
7. Works with Open Educational Resources Coordinator and other librarians to identify, review, and promote open educational resources for teaching and research.
8. Compiles and maintains academic profiles for assigned units. Manages special projects or initiatives related to academic units as assigned.

COLLECTION MANAGEMENT

9. Develops and manages print and electronic collections in assigned areas in accordance with current collection management policies.
10. Manages and reviews approval plan profiles on a regular basis.
11. Manages allocations for the purchase of library materials for assigned subject areas.
12. Works with disciplinary teams and the Director of Collection Management & Scholarly Communication (D/CMSC) to prioritize purchases and coordinate collection management projects as necessary.
13. Participates in library collection review projects.
14. Performs regular assessment to maintain sustainable and usable collections for faculty and students under the direction of the D/CMSC.

RESEARCH SUPPORT

15. Provides research assistance and education on the use of library and related resources to users in person (by appointment) or remotely (via chat, phone, and email).
16. May provide reference assistance to students, faculty and staff at specific service desks.

INSTRUCTION / INFORMATION & DATA LITERACY

17. Teaches instructional sessions within credit courses in assigned departments and/or works with individual students and small groups outside of credit courses.
18. Develops and provides specialized instruction on library and related resources and the literature of a field through classes, group training sessions, and workshops sponsored by the library or related organizations.
19. Conducts tours and orientation sessions for new and prospective students, faculty, and other patrons.
20. Develops and maintains subject and course guides and special topic guides for the library website and appropriate university websites and systems.
21. Develops and maintains open educational resources for use within library and university online venues and in support OU online learning initiatives.

DIGITAL SCHOLARSHIP

22. Collaborates with scholars on advanced research projects or digital scholarship projects as assigned.

23. Participates as a team member in digital scholarship projects as assigned.

OTHER DUTIES

24. Contributes content for the library website.
25. Compiles and submits activity reports and statistics for liaison activities related to research consultations, instructional activities, outreach programs, and other activities in a timely manner into public services statistics system, ensuring accuracy and completeness. Creates reports related to activities as requested.
26. Develops and maintains subject and interdisciplinary knowledge and knowledge of academic librarianship. Keeps abreast of new technologies/trends and how they may apply within academic libraries and to assigned disciplinary fields. Attends and participates in professional and scholarly conferences, workshops, and webinars.
27. Performs special duties as assigned.

BRANCH MANAGEMENT [APPLICABLE TO BRANCH LIBRARY HEADS ONLY]

28. Responsible for the management of the _____ branch library including daily management of library services and operations and supervision of branch staff.
29. Participates in development of library and branch policy. Implements library policies and practices within specific branch.
30. Works with appropriate staff to manage branch library facility.

May 2014

Page 3 of 3

University of Oregon Libraries

Subject Specialists' Roles and Responsibilities

The subject specialist's symbiotic relationship with the university's academic units creates the basis for communication and collaboration between the library and the university community.

Academic units are assigned a subject specialist librarian, who serves as their primary liaison to the Libraries. Subject specialists serve one or more departments, programs or institutes. The University of Oregon Libraries represent a wide range of services linked by our mission to enable teaching and scholarship by creating, collecting, preserving and providing access to information resources. Subject specialists are uniquely positioned within both the library and the academic unit to support scholarly endeavors by providing both traditional library services and by creating collaborative links between faculty and library departments providing specialized assistance with advanced technologies for creating, preserving and disseminating information.

The subject specialist interacts with departmental faculty, staff and a diverse student body to ensure that the information resources provided by the Libraries meet the evolving research needs of the department. They understand and respond to developments in styles of scholarly communication and evolving information technologies relevant to the discipline. Because of the subject specialist\'s involvement with instruction, changes in methodologies and pedagogy are followed and the subject specialist maintains an awareness of issues of information literacy, curricular support, educational technologies, and classroom equipment needs. The subject specialist serves as an advocate for the department within the Libraries, insuring that the Libraries' policies and services are responsive to the needs of the department and researchers within the discipline.

Equally important, the subject specialist represents the Libraries to the department. The subject specialist interprets and promotes the Libraries' collections, services, and policies to students, staff, and faculty. Subject specialists take responsibility for making themselves known and available to the areas they serve, responding to collection, research, instruction, and information technology needs of the department by answering questions and providing services or by making appropriate referrals to other individuals or departments within the Libraries and beyond. Subject specialists' active involvement with their departments expedites collaboration between faculty and Library departments providing specialized services such as faculty instruction and training. advanced classroom and other technologies, new methods of information dissemination and the creation and preservation of information resources.

Subject specialists' activities include:

Communication and Outreach

Although the particular patterns of communication will vary widely depending on individual disciplines and department cultures, subject specialists:

1

- work closely with a departmental representative or departmental faculty committee;
- represent the Libraries at departmental activities ranging from faculty meetings to social events and colloquia;
- communicate with the members of the departmental community, including faculty, graduate and undergraduate students, and staff using avenues appropriate for the department;
- provide appropriate referrals to other experts or service providers within the libraries and across the university;
- interact with faculty doing interdisciplinary work through campus institutes, area studies programs and other cross-disciplinary efforts;
- alert other departments within the Libraries to changing departmental research, program changes, educational technology needs, relevant classroom technology and equipment, special projects requiring advanced technologies or information creation and preservation assistance, faculty training and other needs that may be met by service providers within the Libraries.

Collection Development

Subject specialists have a variety of responsibilities for collection development and assessment in their discipline areas. As part of their Collection Development responsibilities, subject specialists:

- develop an active knowledge of the discipline\'s information resources in all formats within the Libraries' collection as well as those freely available or available for purchase;
- select materials that support diversity and diverse viewpoints, and promote accessible content to students of all backgrounds;
- maintain knowledge of collection strengths of other libraries, both within the area\'s library consortium and within the discipline area;
- understand the department's collection needs and select library materials in support of the curriculum as well as individual research;
- communicate with departments regarding new library materials and research tools;
- collaborate with other subject specialists to build collections and to purchase interdisciplinary resources;
- manage budget lines by utilizing discretionary funds to purchase library materials and by developing, monitoring and updating approval plans;
- maintain active review of serial subscriptions, available formats, and access options in order to provide the best and most efficient access;
- develop knowledge of scholarly communication issues in general and specifically in discipline areas;
- stay abreast of collection access and use issues in order to provide input to library decisions concerning copyright, licensing, preservation, and archiving;
- solicit and manage gift material and funds in collaboration with development officers;
- participate in the formulation of collection development policies;
- evaluate collections for internal use, program reviews or accreditation utilizing available assessment tools.

2

Instruction and Reference

The subject specialist is an integral part of the instructional mission of the University and is an instructional partner with departmental faculty.

The subject specialist works with faculty in developing, delivering and assessing research instruction through course integrated instruction. Subject specialists' reference and instruction responsibilities may include:

- develop course integrated instruction sessions designed to provide general research techniques, help students understand and evaluate diverse viewpoints, reflect particular discipline specific research methods or to explore library research approaches to specific problems or projects;
- provide unique instructional sessions such as workshops, orientations or demonstrations of new resources for groups or individuals in departments, interdisciplinary programs or institutes;
- develop discipline specific credit courses on library and research related topics;
- serve as a resource outside of the classroom;
- create instructional support material including research guides in appropriate formats;
- assess student knowledge of library research and measure student learning from library instruction;
- understand the Libraries' potential role in providing content or support for the department's use of educational technologies, utilizing these tools in library instruction and informing the department of developments in their use;
- utilize discipline knowledge and retrieval skills to contribute to the design and creation of instructional content;
- refer faculty to appropriate library departments for training and lab assistance in educational technologies, classroom equipment and other advanced teaching and research technologies;
- utilize discipline knowledge to connect departments with special teleconferencing and other educational opportunities in the digital environment by expediting collaboration between the academic units and library departments;
- make appropriate referrals to other service providers in the library, on campus and beyond for both instruction and reference.

Reference Service is a strong partner with the instructional duties of the subject specialist. Many subject specialists serve regularly on a public service desk. This experience strengthens instructional expertise and collection development skill by giving insight into how patrons search, the nature of patron questions, instructional needs, and topics of current interest in their subject areas. Subject specialists also provide subject specific, one on one reference assistance outside of their service desk responsibilities.

September 22, 2006
By Cara List, JQ Johnson, Katy Lenn, and Annie Zeidman-Karpinski

3

Liaison Librarian Job Description

At Vanderbilt, professional librarians' job responsibilities are structured around the model of liaison relationships. The liaison model includes the following eight categories. No one individual will simultaneously have major responsibilities in all eight, and the relative priority of various activities will change from year to year. Job descriptions will reference this overall structure, with updates annually to identify and prioritize which components are emphasized in each person's role.

Outreach/Communications

Initiate efforts to seek out and make contact with library constituents within and outside the university; promote the services and resources of the library while cultivating relationships with library stakeholders. Example outreach activities include:

- Develop relationships with university departments, institutes, or sponsored programs; when possible work collaboratively on projects
- Serve on university, college, or school-level committees

Campus Engagement

Participate in campus life beyond the confines of the library's traditional spaces and services; demonstrate the liaison's investment in the larger educational and cultural goals of the universities. Example campus engagement activities include:

- Attend concerts, lectures, athletics, and other campus events
- Involvement with student activities, clubs or the Commons

Teaching and learning

Promote information literacy by educating users on how to find, evaluate, and use information effectively, ethically, and legally. Example teaching and learning activities include:

- Teach course-related and course integrated instructional classes as requested
- Create and develop instruction related materials such as Research Guides.

Reference/Research Services

Provide reference services to library users in a rapidly changing information environment; provide specialized research services to liaison departments. Example reference/research services activities include:

- Provide instruction and assistance in using libraries and their resources through tours, workshops, creation of handouts, Research Guides, and/or tutorials; assistance at a reference point via chat, phone, or email
- Assist library users with managing information

Content/Collection Development and Maintenance

Coordinate with the faculty and students of liaison departments to select and acquire appropriate materials in the most usable formats for the collection. Example content/collection development activities include:

Liaison Librarian Job Description

- Keep up with new developments and apply new strategies for collection development
- Develop metrics to show how the collection supports current scholarship in assigned areas by having conversations with faculty about current research, performing citation analysis, and/or by reading faculty and student publications

Scholarly Communications

Facilitate the dissemination of academic research by fostering emerging communication technologies while reducing legal barriers to access; support students and faculty who are exploring the areas of authors' rights, data curation, digital humanities, electronic theses and dissertations, geographic information systems, learning management systems, open access publishing, and scholarly repositories. Examples of scholarly communications activities include:

- Promote the concept of reproducible research, providing advice to faculty and students about writing data management plans and documenting best practices for data curation
- Educate and inform faculty, graduate students, and campus administrators about the fundamentals of intellectual property law, advocating for authors' rights and promoting the use of permissive copyright licenses

Leadership

Develop and demonstrate ideas or practices that others may want to follow. Examples of leadership activities include:

- Take leadership roles in campus, departmental, or library system-wide committees
- Actively contributes to and participates in professional organizations, sharing insight, knowledge, and skills

Exhibit and Event Planning

Identify and develop events and exhibits that appeal to the senses and promote traditional and non-traditional collections, materials, campus interests and scholarly subjects. Examples of exhibit and event planning include:

- Coordinate or plan events (i.e. Zome competition, open houses, author receptions, mini-golf, scavenger hunts, etc.)
- Participate in the library's exhibition program by working with the Director of Special Projects to curate an exhibit

Program Evolution

Strategic Objective III.1 Formalize the Network of Library Liaisons to Departments and Academic Programs Across the University to Strengthen Relationships. Build Liaisons' Subject and Information Expertise to Enhance Ongoing Dialogue with Researchers.

Final Report

I.   Introduction

In September, 2011, the Library Executive Group (LEG) charged a small team of library staff to work on developing one of the strategic priorities for the Library for the period 2012-2015, i.e. formalizing the network of library liaisons to departments and academic programs.

The team members include:
Kathy Chiang (co-chair)
Virginia Cole
Dan McKee
Fiona Patrick (replaced by Gail Steinhart)
Patrizia Sione
Kornelia Tancheva (co-chair)
Jill Wilson
Drew Wright

The LEG sponsors of the team are Janet McCue and Oya Rieger.

In a discussion with the sponsors, the following goals were set:
- Look at the University's strategic plan goal regarding library services for faculty and build a robust cohesive program around it.
- The program should include, among other things, a table matrix of liaisons, updated job descriptions, clear expectations for liaisons, training for liaisons, means of spreading resources across units; and two-way communication (from library to faculty and from faculty/departments to library).

The team was asked to conclude its work by the end of December 2012.

LEG and the Managers' Council also produced an initial Goal/Objectives/Deliverable Document, which the team revised and is attached at the end of the report as **Appendix 1.**

2

II.   Executive Summary

1.   Environmental Scan of Liaison Activities at CUL

The team completed an environmental scan of the current liaison activities at CUL, which revealed that they are robust and diverse and take into account the specificities of the schools, colleges, and disciplines, the expertise of current liaisons, as well as staffing patterns at each library.

Generally speaking, liaison activities focus on two areas: research support services (including in-depth reference support and instruction) and materials selection. Some liaisons focus on only one of those areas, others on both in various proportions.

Assigning of liaisons varies by library—in some units, one liaison is assigned to multiple departments, in others, all liaisons are assigned to individual faculty, in still others, one liaison is assigned to a department. In rare cases, the liaison responsibilities are shared between a selector and a reference librarian. In departments which reside in multiple schools, more than one liaison is assigned from different libraries. Thus, the number of faculty per liaison varies greatly.

The full environmental scan of the current liaison activities, including conclusions and recommendation, is included as **Appendix 2.**

2.   Environmental Scan of Other Institutions

The team completed an environmental scan of liaison activities at other institutions, which revealed that most liaison programs in polled institutions, with the exception of a few, are informal, fluid, with no dedicated funding, no formal training, and no assessment tools. In all polled institutions, however, significant efforts are underway to maintain strong relationships and share information with the academic communities the libraries serve.

The full environmental scan of other institutions is included as **Appendix 3.**

3.   General Expectations and Suggested Best Practices

Based on the conducted environmental scans and the feedback of the team's LEG sponsors, who identified three areas to focus liaison activities on: reference and instruction; collection development, and scholarly communication, the team compiled documents delineating the general practices (for liaisons who do not work in the specific area) and suggested best practices (for liaisons who do work in the respective specific areas), which are included as **Appendix 4.**

These documents were compiled and revised multiple times after the team gathered feedback from liaisons and library administrators at the Reference and Outreach Forum, selectors' teams (Humanities, Social Sciences, Sciences, Area Team), PSEC, CDExec, individual liaisons, as well as faculty.

9

Appendix 2: Current Liaison Activities at CUL

Based on interviews with unit library directors or their representatives, as well as discussions with the Reference and Outreach Committee, and representatives of Collection Development, Digital Scholarship Services and IT. Examples are provided for illustration and are not meant to be exhaustive.

I.   General Description

The current liaison activities at CUL are robust and diverse and take into account the specificities of the schools, colleges, and disciplines, the expertise of current liaisons, as well as the staffing patterns at each library.

Generally speaking, they focus on two areas: research support services (including in-depth reference support and instruction) and selection. Some liaisons focus on only one of those areas, others on both in various proportions.

Assigning of liaisons varies by library—in some units, one liaison is assigned to multiple departments (e.g. Mann, Vet, Engineering), in others, all liaisons are assigned to individual faculty (e.g. Law, JGSM, ILR, Hotel), in still others, one liaison is assigned to a department (e.g. Olin/Uris, Music, Fine Arts, Math, Africana). In rare cases, the liaison responsibilities are shared between a selector and a reference librarian (e.g. in Philosophy where the selector is in LTS and the reference librarian in Public Services). In departments which reside in multiple schools, more than one liaison may be assigned from different libraries. Thus, the number of faculty per liaison varies greatly.

Certain programs and centers also have liaisons (e.g. Fulbright, Institute for European Studies, Institute for Social Sciences, Society for the Humanities Olin/Uris), Center for Real Estate Finance (Hotel School); Moot Court (Law)).

The virtual libraries (Physical Sciences, Engineering) have pioneered the model of embedded librarians who offer office hours in departments.

Some units also work closely with their School's Administrations (Hotel, JGSM, Vet, Law).

II.   Liaison Activities in the Area of Selection and Collection Development

In the area of selection and collection development, the liaisons who are also selectors, engage in activities such as:

- Building the collections; responding to purchase requests, reviewing cancellations, Annex transfers, etc.; identifying gaps in the collections, securing resources and filling the gaps
- Intelligence gathering; engaging faculty and graduate students; communicating developments and activities
- Provision of alerts on selected subject resources (Africana, Music, Mann, Olin/Uris); new book lists (all); new e-resources updates (PSL; ILR)
- Monthly updates on collections
- Attendance at subject-specific conferences (Math, Olin/Uris, Mann)

10

- Focus on scholarly communication and online publication patterns (Math)

III.   Liaison Activities in the Areas of Research and Instruction

In the area of research and instruction support, the liaisons, who are also reference and instruction librarians, engage in activities such as:

- Research Consultations (all)
- Teaching support (all)
- Faculty paper processing (RMC, Engineering)
- Digital repositories support (e.g. Digital Commons at ILR)
- Compiling profiles with research interests; help with research, including emergency cite checks (Law)
- Liaison for journals (e.g. Law)

IV.   Liaison Activities in the Area of Scholarly Communication

This is the area of greatest variety in the extent to which liaisons engage in it. Some of the reasons might be that it is comparatively newer to the portfolio of library liaisons; that the concerns in scholarly communication manifested at a very different speed in the sciences, the social sciences, and the humanities; as well as the fact that the expertise required in some areas of scholarly communication (e.g. copyright) is very specialized.

V.   Methods of Communication and Engaging with the Academic Community

These vary again depending on the local environment, the needs of the discipline and program, and the library staffing. The following are generally employed:
- Attendance at department events (department meetings, colloquia and seminars: Music, PSL, Engineering, Olin/Uris; job talks: Music, Olin/Uris; forums: Music; formal and informal department gatherings: Physical Sciences)
- Participation in various CU committees and task forces (RMC), school committees (Hotel), department committees (Olin/Uris)
- Participation in faculty hiring process and prospective graduate student recruitment (Olin/Uris, RMC)
- New faculty and graduate student orientation (all)
- Alerts to departments, administrative managers, etc. about services and facilities
- Participation in faculty library boards
- House calls (Vet)
- Participation in graduate students' organized or sponsored events (e.g. graduate reading group: Music; pro-seminars (Olin/Uris) and serving on dissertation committees (Olin/Uris) and as faculty advisors (Law)
- Production of various PR materials: brochures, web sites, blogs by unit (Engineering, Math, PSL; Olin/Uris, Law) and by subject areas (e.g. History, English), digital signs, social media, etc.

VI.   Comments

11

The following general insights and recommendations emerged from the discussions with library directors and outreach coordinators:

- The success of our liaison efforts depends on resources, but also on a chemistry between the department/program and the liaison
- Resources among libraries vary
- Being in the building where the college is makes liaison much easier
- While everyone uses CountIt, only Management is piloting a Customer Management System.
- There is a feeling that not enough information is provided for liaisons on library-wide initiatives.
- Leverage resources across the system to ensure liaison sustainability (e.g. Olin and FA, Mann and Vet)
- Collaborate with other functional units (e.g. DCAPS, Metadata Services, IT) to create a production line behind public services liaison activities
- Provide a consistent level of liaison engagement across the system that is customized for the local audience
- Formalize the liaison program based on department and program affiliation but also on subject areas
- Provide a "best-practices" blue-print for liaisons
- Provide training for liaisons and encourage them to increase subject expertise and knowledge of departments
- Provide regular information on library-wide initiatives for liaisons
- Leverage expertise in areas that span subjects more effectively (e.g. RMC, GIS, data curation, visual resources)
- Make time for liaison activities and make this activity a priority
- Specify expectations, make liaison activities part of the performance dialogue, provide measures of success
- Provide a forum to share the information both with staff in the units and across the system

15

Appendix 4: General Expectations and Suggested Best Practices for Liaisons Documents (final revision Oct. 2012)

Reference and Instruction

Instruction

General expectations for liaisons who are not instruction librarians

- Promote library instruction
- Know about the Library Instruction web site: ttp://www.library.cornell.edu/svcs/serve/classinst
- Be familiar with the dimensions of the library instruction program---including course-integrated, customized library research sessions at the undergraduate as well as graduate level, workshops on topics like images and citation management, orientation for new graduate students in a given department, etc.
- Be aware of current information literacy developments
- Be aware of the efforts of unit instruction coordinator(s) and the PSEC Instruction Committee to promote library instruction, etc.
- Serve as a communication conduit between faculty and the library regarding their existing and evolving needs for Instruction services and tools
- Be able to refer instruction issues and requests to appropriate unit instruction coordinator(s)

Suggested best practices for liaisons who are instruction librarians include:

- Maintain regular contact with department/program including directors of undergraduate studies and the directors of graduate studies to learn about curriculum and discuss instruction issues
- Examine the schedule of classes each semester; identity core/foundational, research methods, and capstone courses, contacting appropriate faculty
- Analyze department curriculum; identify and target critical courses for library instruction and work with the pertinent faculty
- Deliver effective instruction which includes class sessions and other mechanisms such as LibGuides, individual research consultations, online tutorials, handouts, etc.
- Develop plans and strategies to deliver effective instruction for target populations
- Develop instructional programs and learning materials in a variety of formats, using instructional design principles
- Engage in reflective teaching through use of instructional improvement tools such as attending forums, discussion groups, workshops, speakers, and peer evaluation, etc.
- Attend workshops and other activities organized by the Instruction Committee
- Create student learning outcomes for library instruction sessions, assess learning, and use assessment to improve instruction and student learning
- Identify, explore, and use new technologies to enhance student learning, as appropriate

16

- Engage faculty and other teaching staff in order to integrate information literacy concepts and skills into the curriculum.

Reference Services

General expectations for liaisons who are not reference librarians

- Promote reference services and Ask a Librarian
- Be aware of hours and staffing, and current formats and scope of reference service
- Serve as a communication conduit between faculty and the library regarding their existing and evolving needs for reference services and tools
- Be able to make referrals to appropriate reference staff

Suggested best practices for liaisons who are reference librarians include:

- Maintain regular contact with department/program to learn about researchers' needs and discuss research support issues
- Be proficient in effective catalog and database searching, finding sources, requesting materials, citation style, current alerts, citation management, information management, technical troubleshooting, etc.
- Keep current with new databases, resources, technologies, library discovery systems, library web site design, etc.
- Attend reference training sessions
- Answer questions fully and knowledgeably
- Participate in staffing of reference desk, email, phone, chat, and/or text a Librarian
- Provide research consultations

Scholarly Communications

General expectations for liaisons who are not experts in scholarly communication

- Be familiar with emerging issues (e.g., open access mandates) and programs (e.g., A&S grants, Cornell Open Access Publication fund) in scholarly communication.
- Be familiar with resources and service points to assist with intellectual property rights issues, including copyright, fair use and plagiarism.
- Promote use of institutional and subject repositories and foster a better understanding of open access and new models of scholarly communication.
- Engage faculty and teaching staff regarding digital media creation opportunities.
- Be sufficiently informed of issues related to data management in order to make appropriate referrals to the Research Data Management Service Group (RDMSG) or other experts.
- Serve as a communication conduit between faculty and the library regarding their existing and evolving needs for scholarly communications services and tools

17

- Be able to refer scholarly communication issues and requests to the appropriate service providers

Suggested best practices for liaisons who are scholarly communication experts Include:

- Maintain regular contact with department/program to learn about researchers' needs and discuss scholarly communication issues
- Develop familiarity with CUL's repositories (such as eCommons, Mann Locale, arXiv, DigitalCommons@ILR, and SharedShelf) and service points to provide preliminary information and referrals to faculty/researchers.
- Maintain current awareness of data management trends and issues (data management plan requirements, sharing research data) and promote awareness of policies that pertain to research data (funders' requirements, IPR, privacy, confidentiality).
- Build awareness of Cornell/CUL programs that support open access and sustainable publishing, such as the Cornell Open Access Publication (COAP) fund, and direct interested researchers to the appropriate contacts.
- Facilitate the implementation of new policies (such as the 2007 NIH public access policy) by informing faculty of them and related CUL support services.
- Identify needs for continuing copyright and IPR education and refer those to copyright services as appropriate.
- Identify potential needs for digital content creation and collaborate with digital media service providers on subsequent project development and management.

- Seek partnerships with faculty on digitization initiatives such as the ones funded by the A&S grants.
- Promote awareness of best practices and available services for digitization and archiving of personal holdings

Collection Development

General expectations for liaisons who are not selectors:

- Be aware of faculty and graduate student research interests and needs
- Be familiar with collections and appropriate collection development policies
- Be familiar with current publishing trends
- Be familiar with CUL's collections fundraising initiatives
- Be aware of gift policies
- Be aware of cooperative partnerships, such as 2CUL
- Serve as a communication conduit between faculty and the library regarding their existing and evolving needs for collection development services and tools
- Be able to refer collection development issues and requests to the appropriate selector(s)

18

Suggested best practices for liaisons who are selectors include:

- Maintain regular contact with department/program to learn about researchers' needs and discuss collection development issues
- Develop, monitor and analyze collections to support advanced researcher's subject areas
- Build and maintain relationships with faculty and other researchers, including participating in joint projects, and inform them of new resources in their areas of interest, including electronic databases and other research tools
- Participate in the department/program activities, as appropriate to discipline and specific library's policies and expectations
- Build relationships with donors, including communicating with endowment fund donors, working with Library Development, and assisting in the gift process
- Communicate with colleagues inside and outside Cornell to seek opportunities to pool funds and share resources where appropriate, and coordinate related efforts
- Follow "Competences for Selectors" established by CDExec (http://www.library.cornell.edu/colldev/cdcompetences.html)

UNIVERSITY of **HOUSTON** | **LIBRARIES**

LIAISON SERVICES

Strategic Document

INTRODUCTION & BACKGROUND

The Liaison Services Department developed this strategic document in the summer of 2013 with revisions in summer 2014. It maintains the Mission, Vision, and revised Values from the departmental documents that guided our work from 2011 to 2013, but provides a new set of goals for 2014-2015.

All members of the Liaison Services Department contributed to this document by participating in facilitated discussions about our departmental values, a SWOT analysis, brainstorming sessions based on the UH Libraries new 2013-16 Strategic Directions and the university's Tier One initiatives, and a conversation about our definition of success for the department. The department heads and Liaison Leadership Team reviewed the results of these activities and synthesized them into a single document.

Our department's 2014-15 goals align closely with the university priorities of National Recognition, particularly for research, and Student Success, as well as with the UH Libraries' Strategic Directions, especially "Target Specific User Groups with Customized Services and Niche Collections" and "Promote UH Libraries with a Consistent Message and a Focused Outreach Strategy."

The goals also include two departmental values we seek to highlight and enhance this year, Internal Collaboration and Accountability, and include under the umbrella of Liaison Services the goals of two committees whose membership goes beyond the department, the Instruction Management Committee (IMC) and the Collection Management Committee (CMC). We have included these areas in our departmental goals in order to encourage Liaison Services members to thoughtfully consider how their work can uphold two especially important departmental values and to establish stronger relationships between the department and the committees that oversee two of the functional areas for which liaison librarians are responsible.

Mission

What We Do & Why

The liaison services department connects the campus community with quality information and library services, engages in academic conversation across campus, and contributes to the scholarly community in order to advance the teaching and research mission of the university.

Vision

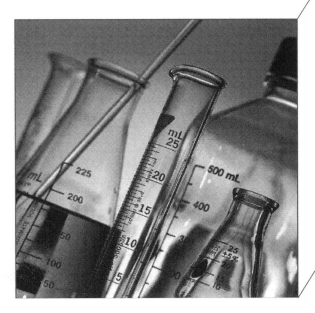

What We Aspire To Do

We aspire to empower all UH students to inquire about and discover the power of information and new possibilities.

We aspire to be a creative partner with faculty and staff to facilitate innovative teaching, student success, and research productivity.

Values

How We Conduct Ourselves

Campus Relationships

We believe building connections and relationships across campus increases the visibility of library services and increases the success of students and faculty.

Expertise

We have expertise that contributes to teaching and research, and we strive to partner with campus stakeholders to advance the mission of the university.

User-Centered

Our services and initiatives are based on user needs. We will ask why a service or imitative is needed; consider its value; apply research, data, or assessment; discuss opportunities it affords our users, and plan for how we will measure its success. We will not let this inhibit our ability to move quickly, but rather, we use this to test how well we have thought through our ideas..

Continual Improvement

We are willing to improve and invest in new ideas learned from one another, collaborators, and professional activities.

Internal Collaboration

We work in teams to leverage expertise, both within the department and throughout the UH Libraries, in order to strengthen our ability to achieve our vision and goals.

Accountability

Out of respect for each other and the work we do, and in order to provide the highest possible level of service to the campus community, we hold ourselves and our colleagues accountable for meeting goals, expectations, and commitments. We believe in openly communicating about accountability and we will seek and offer feedback to help hold ourselves accountable.

Emotional Intelligence

As a department we seek to improve our relationships, communication, and organizational culture by committing to a shared effort of self-improvement and self-reflection around all attributes of emotional intelligence.

Liaison Services
Goals 2014-2015

Focus On Values

Internal Collaboration:

- Communicate our goals to stakeholders and UH Libraries collaborators
- Balance our pursuits with other departmental priorities
- Work to help other departments meet goals when possible

Accountability:

- Be more purposeful about sharing and following through on training and learning opportunities
- Build documentation procedures into projects
- Continue to assess at least 50% library instruction sessions, and focus on making positive changes by turning our assessment feedback into action

Graduate Student Support

- Develop a sustainable, comprehensive model for a workshop series focused on knowledge and skills needed to be successful as researchers and teachers.
- Create and implement a program to market current services and resources to graduate students across colleges. Make recommendations on how this program can be sustainable.

Outreach & Research Support

- Create a solid foundation for expanding our data-related services by building relationships, awareness, and infrastructure, both internally (within the Libraries) and externally (on campus and in the community).
- Determine our core services as a department and develop a method to identify department members with particular skills or expertise and ensure appropriate intra-departmental collaboration.

Instruction

- Develop a comprehensive online learning plan to address a growing expansion of online courses.
- Using the new ACRL IL Framework and the curriculum mapping project results, create programmatic learning outcomes and strategies.
- Continue to assess and change lower level modules and instructional approaches, keeping in mind the new IL Framework.

Collections

- Continue to align collections activities, especially the acquisition of new resources, with university priorities, as indicated by new degree programs, faculty hires, increasing enrollments, etc. Specifically, determine a methodology for general prioritization of subject areas.
- To ensure close alignment with university priorities and good stewardship of our resources, continue collection assessment processes, including implementing changes based on recent collection assessment projects.

KU Libraries' Consultant Model

Recommended actions for implementation

Erin Ellis, Judith Emde and Beth Whittaker—June 23, 2014

APPENDIX A

KU Libraries Consultant Model
July 2013

In May 2013, KU Libraries' executive leadership commissioned the development of a consultant model sufficiently agile to respond to an ever evolving research and learning landscape. It was determined that the Libraries' liaison model, in which an individual librarian performed an array of duties in reference, collection development, instruction, and department-specific outreach, could not be reliably sustained. While the liaison model has been a key to the Libraries' past success, with changing emphases of the University's goals and a need to reaffirm the Libraries' contribution to the University's mission, a different model was deemed necessary to meet the complex needs of our patrons. The Libraries' executive leadership felt it must reposition and re-concentrate the expertise of its faculty and staff in order to meet emerging user needs and expectations and to address significant Libraries and campus-level strategic initiatives.

KU Libraries executive leadership appointed three Assistant Deans--Erin Ellis of Research & Learning, Judith Emde of Content & Access, and Beth Whittaker of Distinctive Collections--to develop a consultant model for KU Libraries. Over the course of 10 meetings between May 30 and July 10, this group examined many issues related to the conceptual model of a consultant in a user-centered organization and the attendant implementation issues, and reflected on feedback received from Libraries employees through informal conversation and emails, and through consultation with other stakeholders. The group agreed that the Libraries would be best served by a general "canopy" model that could be applied to all consultants within the organization, with the understanding that the manifestation and expectations associated with consultant work will necessarily vary across divisions.

Who are consultants?

Consultants will be the Libraries' faculty and professional staff members who cultivate and maintain relationships through proactive, regular engagement with KU faculty and students, as well as our Kansas community and affiliates, in support of research, teaching and learning.

What will consultants do?

Consultants will be tasked with outreach to their appropriate constituencies to the benefit of KU Libraries and its strategic initiatives. The specific consultation activities performed by consultants are dependent upon the division in which the consultant is based; the fundamental expectations associated with consultation in each division will be determined by the respective Assistant Dean and department heads.

How does the Consultant Model differ from the Liaison model?

As the Libraries transitions into its new organizational structure, many duties formerly performed in the course of liaison work will be assigned to dedicated personnel, allowing staff to concentrate on their

11

principal area of responsibility. The anticipated timeline for major components of this transition include:

- By July 2014, Research & Learning and Content Development personnel will transition away from primary performance of reference desk duties, except where specific expertise is requested
- By July 2015, Content Development personnel will transition away from primary performance of instruction duties, except where specific expertise is requested
- By July 2015, Research & Learning personnel will transition away from content development duties

Therefore, with this redistribution of work, the consultant model will focus on the performance of consistently effective and relevant collaboration, outreach, and relationship building with KU faculty and students. The consultant model is also highly reliant upon coordinated application of expertise from across the Libraries' divisions and throughout all levels of the organization.

How will the transition to the consultant model proceed?

In the immediate future, those who performed actively in the former liaison role should:
- Continue to field questions from KU departments, while also referring to appropriate Libraries personnel (e.g., Content Development; Office of Scholarly Communication & Copyright; etc.)

- Faculty and staff within Content Development and Research & Learning will facilitate the transition process by consulting with John Stratton (Center of Undergraduate Initiatives) or Scott McEathron (Center for Graduate Initiatives) on instruction requests in order to determine the best route of instruction.

In the future, general campus announcements will be coordinated through the Centers, in consultation with the Office of Communications & Advancement. The Centers will solicit Libraries' departments for content. Libraries staff can continue to contact KU departments and schools with questions and announcements specific to their areas.

Because faculty and professionals in Content Development and Research & Learning eventually will not be scheduled for the Anschutz and Watson reference desks, for those questions requiring in-depth assistance, subject and service specialists will be contacted. A referral list with contact information will be developed and maintained.

With the Libraries' web site currently being updated through a content management system, the Libraries will place a prominent emphasis on the "Ask a Librarian" feature. This service will assist in referring to the appropriate staff member. Training and assessment will be key in ensuring appropriate referrals.

Additionally, KU Libraries leadership will be in conversation with the Assessment Team of the Strategy & Innovation Division to discern the best process for assessing the efficacy of this new model overall and guiding alterations as necessary based upon assessment findings.

12

APPENDIX B

KU Libraries' Consultant Model: moving toward implementation
May 2014

Soon after the reorganization in 2013, the Libraries' administration established an effort toward a consultant model that would better enable the Libraries to respond to an ever-evolving academic landscape. Ensuring our future relevance requires the Libraries to recast how we approach services to our users; we will focus on identifying and meeting the core research and information needs of the user, regardless of the discipline from which that user comes.

In the initial development of the consultant model, a two-year timeline for transitions of duties was established:

- By July 2014, Research & Learning and Content Development personnel will transition away from performance of reference desk duties, except where specific expertise is requested
- By July 2015, Content Development personnel will transition away from performance of instruction duties, except where specific expertise is requested
- By July 2015, Research & Learning personnel will transition away from content development duties

Much of the work of transitioning is already well underway. In as much as possible, the time to complete these transitions is now, in order to address key issues raised during the focus group sessions and prepare for a fall 2014 implementation.

What follows is set of considerations, developed by Assistant Deans Erin Ellis, Judith Emde and Beth Whittaker, for defining the role of expertise in content development, instruction and reference, and moving us closer to implementation of the consultant model. In order to formulate the most effective transition to the consultant model, these ADs are seeking ideas and feedback about the successful implementation of this transition from KU Libraries' faculty and staff.

<u>EXPERTISE</u>

Expertise, both subject and functional, is currently widely distributed across the Libraries and it will continue to be so. Subject expertise will continue to reside primarily within Content Development, for the purpose of building and maintaining collections. Functional expertise is distributed among several areas. The types of expertise and the distribution thereof are outlined below.

<u>Content Development</u>

- History
- Art (visual art and history of art) and architecture
- Music (performing arts)
- English literature

13

- Language proficiency (French, German, Italian)

Metadata, Data & Discovery Services

- Data
- Metadata

Research & Learning

- GIS
- Government documents
- Scholarly Communication & Copyright
- Statistics

Distinctive Collections

- Formats (archives, rare books, conservation of materials)
- Languages

INSTRUCTION

We will no longer approach course support with only a 'subject expertise' frame, but instead will begin with an analysis of what the research/information component of the course is (or could be). Every request for instruction will require a consultation that seeks answers to the following:

1. What is research/information need, regardless of the subject designation or course prefix?
2. What are the learning outcomes?
3. By what methods might the Libraries integrate and help achieve those learning outcomes?
4. Finally, determine whether disciplinary subject expertise or functional expertise is required to meaningfully contribute.
   - Is it an expertise that the professor/instructor can bring to bear through consultation? OR
   - Can a library colleague possessing a subject or functional expertise assist?

100-level courses (with the exception of UNIV 101, HNRS 190, and FYS 177 courses)

- In most cases, requests will be referred to LibGuides and online tutorials.

ENG 101/102

- New model of integration forthcoming: train the trainer in ENG 801/802 courses

14

Our strategic approach to instruction beyond the 100-level is currently under consideration and development. But, as noted above, subject and functional expertise will be sought as appropriate with these courses.

REFERRALS

Because the Libraries is shifting away from framing our services in terms of subject and discipline, the referral model will be recast and simplified over the course of summer 2014. If reference staff find themselves at a point of referral, they will refer based upon:

- Rare formats/collections—Spencer
- Selected languages—International Area Studies
- User population--Centers

Referrals for the purpose of problem-resolution (e.g., fines questions, e-resource problems) will continue to be directed to the parties charged with resolving those issues.

REFERENCE SERVICE in Watson and Anschutz Libraries

Due to declining number of questions posed and need to shift staff to strategic priorities, we are moving to a support staff and student model for providing direct research help in Anschutz and Watson. Anschutz and Watson Libraries will maintain a research help presence at the service desks. All Libraries faculty, as well as staff from Research and Learning, will be removed from reference service at the desks by summer 2014.

QUESTIONS

1. In terms of these recommendations, and from your perspective within the organization, how do you think this transition can be best facilitated? What do you need in order to successfully make this transition?
2. Given that we are shifting from framing our services in terms of subject and discipline, how do you believe the Libraries can best manage the development and maintenance of LibGuides?
3. We recognize that some reference and instruction work may require specialized subject knowledge, due to the complexity of the associated resources. How can the Libraries manage this potential need, understanding the scope of subject expertise in the organization?

15

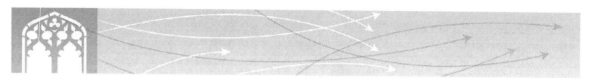

ORGANIZATIONAL RECOMMENDATIONS

RESEARCH AND LEARNING DIVISION

Liaison Model

Some two years ago in June 2011, the consultants retained by the libraries noted, "The liaison role is not well defined, nor does staff view it as flexible. While a variety of approaches exist, mixed results in faculty outreach coupled with communicating the results of that outreach, hamper organizational effectiveness" (Lougee and Luce, 2011).

The consultants also noted there was "uneven engagement" among liaisons and departments and that greater "clarity was needed for position definitions..." (Lougee and Luce, 2011, p. 3).

Not long after the consultants' report was submitted, an internal libraries task force was formed called *Connecting to KU Teaching & Research Departments*, which submitted recommendations to the libraries' administration in September 2010. That report recognized the libraries deliver services to departments along a "continuum of multiple [liaison] models," but assessment of the libraries' efforts revealed several service gaps that warranted greater attention. For example, the task force noted the libraries' use aspects of the "traditional departmental liaison model," the "embedded knowledge model," and the "resource team model," none of which delivered a full suite of services to teaching and research departments on campus (Connecting to KU..., 2010, pp. 5-7). Indeed, several gaps in the models used to serve departments were noted, including these:

- knowledge of scholarly communications and trends
- instruction and research support
- data/collections resources and services
- assessment
- technology skills
- marketing/outreach

While "next steps" were proposed to address such gaps, no further action was taken at that time. Subsequently, there was no organizational consensus reached regarding the role of subject liaisons following either the consultants visit or the work of the internal task force.

Mindful of these efforts, ORT discussed the notion of liaisons and liaison models several times during the fall semester. It should be noted, however, that ORT had only three library faculty as members, not all of whom currently serve as traditional "liaisons." Focus group discussions did not add much clarity to questions surrounding the current liaison model, and the team did not reach consensus regarding whether or not subject specialist designations should be retained in the newly proposed structure.

Notwithstanding that, ORT recommends the designation "liaison" be discontinued and that a new model of outreach be considered and renamed. It may be advisable, for example, to refer to these specialists as "consultants" or some other name. The term "liaison" is based on an older model that stressed collection development, reference, and instruction as the primary responsibilities of all liaisons, no matter the discipline served. Within this context, liaisons were assigned specific disciplines to serve and developed established and formal relationships with departments, schools, or centers across campus. At times, these units work closely with faculty assigned as their library liaison (not all academic units have faculty liaisons).

ORGANIZATIONAL RECOMMENDATIONS

It is true this has aided immensely in the establishment of positive relations with faculty, albeit in an inconsistent way. It is also true that librarians have often formed a close identification with the departments and disciplines they serve. In our current milieu, however, ORT believes our needs have rendered this arrangement insufficient to meet contemporary user expectations. Even now, for example, this model has been informally modified; while most liaisons continue to teach, a cohort of librarians designated as liaisons no longer perform either collection development work and/or reference duties at either Anschutz or Watson service desks, instead preferring to specialize in other areas (such as instruction). Other librarians who perform extensive outreach and instruction with a variety of faculty are not officially considered "liaisons" since they have no formal affiliation with academic units on campus. This is true of the library faculty in CDS, for example.

Our current model, created a number of years ago, has not evolved in parallel with the needs of our users. It is largely uneven in how it is approached by liaisons themselves and in the expectations placed upon individual liaisons by faculty supervisors. It is, in short, a model that is no longer sustainable.

As ORT discussed these issues, the team began to realize librarians and staff must be realigned and become more conversant in 21st century fluencies required for the job. Many of these characteristics were noted by both the consultants and the libraries' own task force created over two years ago. Emphasis should be placed more heavily on building relationships, not strictly on functions to be performed within a narrow range of choices. There exists now the real possibility to build cross-functional teams that better serve our users. The idea of "embedded" librarians involved in both teaching and research, for example, is one idea that could be further developed, but this will require greater explication and could influence whether some subject specialist designations be retained (Schumaker, 2012).

In light of these observations, ORT recognizes the following scenarios could exist:

- Subject specialists could be retained with roles and expectations explicitly defined.
- Subject specialists could be retained for the professional schools (e.g., engineering, social welfare, education, business, journalism, etc.). In addition, librarians in International Area Studies (IAS) should continue to be considered specialists in line with extant university centers on campus, such as those for East Asian and Latin American Studies.
- Current subject specialists could be distributed across the spectrum of administrative units and teams based on preference and need, or those with current subject specialization could be tapped to continue to teach upper-level courses in areas they now do (viz., political science, history, psychology, and so on).

ORT recommends that we at least define responsibilities within the structure proposed in this report: librarians and staff be redistributed to various departments and units (or centers and teams) within Research and Learning, Content Discovery and Access, and Assessment Services, for example. This will better support the activities and priorities that comprise the strategic plan.

As has been noted in the library literature, realignment along the lines we suggest "will have significant implications for the library's staffing profile and workforce skill set" (Luce, 2008). An explicit and ongoing effort should be enacted to enable current library staff in all relevant areas to learn and develop the skills and expertise required to support research and learning in the today's environment.

ORGANIZATIONAL RECOMMENDATIONS

User-based Approach

Currently, the functions of research support, teaching support, and learning support are all handled separately and with little coordination amongst them within the libraries. There is a focus on library functions and workflows or library services, rather than a more explicit focus on the user and user support. Libraries are uniquely situated to build research and learning communities that are multidisciplinary and reach across and beyond institutional boundaries. ORT recommends a user-based structure that echos our commitment to integrating KU Libraries into the academic life of scholars and students--not the other way around (i.e., the traditional model whereby scholars and students must find ways to integrate with the libraries).

The Research and Learning division (R&L) will be comprised of librarians and library staff who possess expertise in a range of areas and topics related to resource discovery and use, teaching and learning, and research. These faculty and staff will provide support to our major constituencies on campus in each of these areas based on distinct user needs, skills, and experiences. These librarians will engage users and build relationships based on both the commonalities and differences that exist among these constituencies. This support will require engaging fundamentally in the lives of students, scholars, and citizens to improve individual productivity and further their academic goals, as well as the mission of the university. "An engagement model is a model that seeks to enhance scholar productivity, empower learners, and integrate libraries into the research, teaching, and learning processes" (Williams, 2009).

Compared to our current organizational structure, the integration of instruction- and research-focused services into one division will exemplify that research and learning are not independent and distinct activities, but two interrelated aspects of the larger scholarly enterprise. As noted above, CDS is engaging in an increasing number of instructional activities with faculty and students, and issues such as open access, scholarly communication, and digital scholarship should be a part of the information literacies of undergraduates, graduates, and researchers. Similarly, it is with increasing frequency that library and research instruction lead to questions and conversations related to copyright, fair use, and the rapidly changing resource and information environment.

Why a user-focused, team-based structure?

A user-focused, cross-functional team-based, organizational structure presents a number of advantages.

Academic institutions distinguish among undergraduates, graduates, and faculty in nearly every respect, and these groupings are not likely to change on the whole. There is a reason for this: each possesses distinct characteristics, skills, and needs.

- **Undergraduates**: are primarily students and novice researchers
- **Graduates**: represent a mix of advanced students, advanced researchers/scholars, and some are also teachers
- **Faculty**: are primarily teachers and expert researchers/scholars
- **Community**: represent a mixed group of local, state, regional, and international users with a variety of information and research needs

ORGANIZATIONAL RECOMMENDATIONS

A user-focused Research and Learning division organized around these four user groups will be a bold break from a (very) traditional organizational structure that has "focused largely on capturing the end products of scholarship and a bibliographer model designed to fulfill that goal" (Williams, 2009). This traditional structure has also made us less agile and less responsive to evolving student learning outcomes, student and faculty research processes, and scholarly communication practices (Hahn, 2009). A user-based focus will bring users to the fore of our attention and may lead to critical strategic opportunities to participate in and influence a variety of campus decisions. It will emphasize our interest in building relationships, explicitly requiring agility and responsiveness, and will best situate us to demonstrate the value and contribution we make to the research, teaching, and learning experiences of our users.

> Building strong relationships with faculty and other campus professionals, and establishing collaborative partnerships within and across institutions will be necessary building blocks to our success. Subject knowledge, such as liaisons possess, can be used to inform much more than the selection of books and journals, and teaching the occasional guest lecture. Knowing how scholars in particular disciplines communicate and share information with one another can inform the design and development of repository and new model publishing services. Understanding the curriculum of a degree program and pedagogical norms of a discipline can help shape the development of scalable models that integrate 21st century literacies into a learner's universe. Knowing that many scholars are generating untold quantities of digital data while others are producing multimedia works and all are struggling with data management and preservation plans positions us to help craft solutions to these large-scale problems (Williams and Jaguscewski, 2012).

We also believe an organization based around user needs and cross-functional teams will make the most effective use of our expert human resources and eliminate several areas of duplication of effort. Given a sure future of limited resources, this is a model in which we can be very effective. A team-based approach to our functional work means we can take advantage of the natural strengths and interests of our staff while not expecting that each individual librarian acquire new specialized skills or expertise in specific areas.

> [Librarians] cannot be experts themselves in each new capability, but knowing when to call in a colleague, or how to describe appropriate expert capabilities to faculty, will be key…Just as researchers are often working in teams to leverage compatible expertise,…librarians will need to be team builders among library experts [where this supports and enhances the research, teaching, and learning on our campus] (Hahn, 2009).

Cross-functional teams also reflect the true nature of our work. While this kind of collaboration currently happens in an ad hoc way (with varying degrees of success), a user-focused structure that utilizes cross-functional teams would provide a structure clearly and explicitly intended to break down our current 'silos' or tribal tendencies and support the kind of ongoing and in-depth collaboration our work requires.

This kind of realignment is also a strategic response to economic realities and pressures. In realigning the libraries' priorities and structuring our focus on the changing needs of faculty and students, we will better equip ourselves to meet current and future needs, and will be best situated to demonstrate direct value and contribution to the research, teaching, and learning experiences of our users.

ORGANIZATIONAL RECOMMENDATIONS

Centers

We recommend a user-based structure for the R&L division comprised of four centers overseeing a number of cross-functional teams. The centers will provide vision, oversight, and coordination to the teams, with an emphasis on engagement and support. They will need to allocate, shift, and share resources (including staff time) among each other, as functional needs will overlap. We recommend director-level leadership of these centers. The center directors will need to collaboratively ensure that user needs are being met and user support is provided efficiently and effectively. Centers are listed below, then described in more detail in the following section:

The Center for Faculty Initiatives and Engagement

Faculty...are the single greatest challenge facing the modern research and academic library. Without faculty support and understanding and without their regular collaboration with librarians, the research library will not survive. It may remain as an interesting museum piece or storage facility, but it will no longer be the heart of the institution.

But the opposite is also true: If we can get faculty and scholars to be willing and eager collaborators with librarians in their course development, teaching, and research, then we will have guaranteed the active and irreplaceable role of the library in higher education, no matter how many books are digitized or how much shelf space is given over to cafés.

Sadly, the exclusion of librarians in both undergraduate course development and advanced scholarship has created a climate in which librarians find themselves struggling to explain their role in research and teaching even to university administrators (Rentfrow, 2008).

The Center for Faculty Initiatives and Engagement will focus on supporting KU's faculty and research community, including KU's research centers, through collaboration and engagement in teaching and research support. Our user-based approach will help KU Libraries develop and articulate its role in supporting the research and teaching within the university. This center (in close collaboration with other centers) will provide higher level coordination and resources to support specialized and cross-functional teams in areas such as Research Data and GIS Services, Digital Research and Publishing, and Scholarly Communications and Copyright.

ORGANIZATIONAL RECOMMENDATIONS

The Center for Graduate Initiatives and Engagement

The Center for Graduate Initiatives and Engagement will focus on the libraries' integration with graduate students in their roles as advanced students, researchers, teachers, and academics and professionals in training. Graduate student needs overlap with both undergraduates and faculty, and they have their own unique situation as early career (or soon-to-be) academics and professionals. This center will engage with the needs of graduate students to ensure that they develop skills and knowledge about not only where to find information and how to evaluate it, but also about how to extract and then manipulate the material they find.

Working in conjunction with graduate students' programs and departments, the center will also provide hands-on experience through internships, employment, project-based initiatives, and other opportunities. The libraries provides a rich environment for the type of "field" experience that graduate curriculums in the humanities find increasingly valuable. Through collaborative, real-world projects, the libraries can provide students opportunities to contribute to scholarly projects and build skills in areas such as digital humanities, interdisciplinary team-based work, and teaching. Such an initiative would increase KU Libraries' viability by strengthening our connection to the larger KU graduate curriculum, building the skills and qualifications of the students graduating from KU, and clearly demonstrating our long-term value to the university.

The Center for Graduate Initiatives and Engagement will allow KU Libraries to focus on these initiatives to a far greater degree, and with far greater coordination, than we have been able to do up to this point.

The Center for Undergraduate Initiatives and Engagement

The Center for Undergraduate Initiatives and Engagement will focus on supporting undergraduate teaching and learning through collaboration with teaching faculty and first-year experience offices, and through the design of undergraduate programs and outreach from the libraries. KU has made a commitment to the undergraduate experience in *Bold Aspirations*, and the Center for Undergraduate Initiatives and Engagement will ensure that KU Libraries develops and articulates its role in supporting that commitment. Further, the libraries' strategic plan also calls for the coordination of efforts in support of undergraduate teaching and learning. This center (in close collaboration with other centers) will provide high level coordination and resources to support specialized and cross-functional teams such as Course and Curriculum Integration/Teaching Support; Outreach; Online and Distance Learning Support; Discovery, Access, and Use; Student Learning Support; and First Year Experience Initiatives.

The Center for Community and Affiliate Initiatives and Engagement

The Center for Community and Affiliate Initiatives and Engagement will focus on supporting the varied needs of our community members and KU affiliates. Presently, this kind of engagement is not done in any organized or coordinated manner. This center will ensure that we are considering the needs of our users, regardless of location. *Bold Aspirations* calls upon members of the KU community to reach out to our fellow Kansans in a variety of ways, but also to raise our collective profile at the national and international levels. Through collaboration with alumni, the *KU Works for Kansas* initiative, and our colleagues at other Kansas institutes of higher education, this center will develop partnerships and provide the necessary resources and services to these community members and affiliates. This center (in close collaboration with other centers) will provide high level coordination and resources to support specialized and cross-functional teams in areas such as Outreach; Online and Distance Learning Support; and Discovery, Access, and Use.

KU Libraries: Organizational Review Team Report

37

UMass Amherst Libraries Librarian Engagement Framework: moving forward

The Liaison Advisory Council ("LAC") developed the attached document over the past couple of months. The purpose of it is to serve as an internal document to guide UMass librarians. The Framework intentionally broadens staff involved in what we currently refer to as the "Liaison Program" because the suite of services and expertise the Libraries offers has grown beyond the 'liaison program' paradigm as it has been described up to this point

Librarians have had the opportunity to review and comment on the document. When reviewing it, librarians were asked to note if their work activities are reflected in the document—and if not to inform the LAC so they may be added. Numerous additions and revisions have been made based on the feedback received, with the goal that all UMass Amherst librarians will see themselves in the Framework.

The document will serve as a guide for the Librarian Engagement Framework, once SMG has approved it. It will be reviewed on a yearly basis by the LAC.

Members of Liaison Advisory Council:

Marilyn Billings
Leslie Button
Carol Connare
Rob Cox
Kate Freedman
Beth Lang (co-chair)
Maxine Schmidt (co-chair)
Brian Shelburne
Gabe Stetson
Christine Turner

The UMass Amherst Libraries Librarian Engagement Framework

UMass Amherst Libraries Liaison Program: moving forward

The Liaison Advisory Council ("LAC") developed this document to serve as an internal guide to UMass Librarians who serve in what we what we currently refer to as the **Liaison Program.**
The new name of this specific group, now to be called the **Librarian Engagement Program,** reflects the Library's goal to reach out and to actively participate in supporting teaching, learning, and research efforts across the University campus. It is our intention, as well, that all UMass Amherst librarians and staff will see themselves and their roles described to some extent, somewhere in this document; that all will identify with the values articulated here and will participate, to the extent that is appropriate, in the broad range of activities described.

Background

Academic libraries have become more complex, offering services that are more diverse and responsive to the significant changes that are affecting higher education. Academic libraries have re-oriented the subject specialist/liaison librarian cohort from the traditional collections-focused role to a teaching/learning and research enterprise role. This new model requires a more collaborative, engaged approach that builds on expertise from across *all units* in the UMass Amherst Libraries (Libraries) to blend librarian expertise more integrally into the teaching/learning workflow, institutional objectives, and research practices of scholars, researchers, and students.

While we continue to provide traditional library support to faculty and students, we also now assist users in interpreting the increasingly complex information infrastructure, of which the Libraries are part.We are already actively engaged in the teaching, learning, and research enterprise. In so doing, we play an important role in facilitating collaboration and collective action across disciplinary and institutional boundaries.

Framework Purpose and Structure

The Framework foci below are intended as both a guide and a toolkit for librarians serving the UMass Amherst community, defined as faculty, students, staff, and citizens of the Commonwealth. It describes prospective librarian roles based on the Libraries' and the University's strategic plans. Librarians are expected to use the Framework foci as a guide to identify opportunities, priorities, and specific activities for respective constituencies.

The document consists of two main sections: the Values and the Outline. The Values apply to all librarians, regardless of home department or functional role. The Outline describes responsibilities and expectations along with 'best practice examples' to inform implementation strategies for core engagement activities. These 'best practice examples' are not comprehensive. The purpose of the Outline is to both give ideas about how to implement the program, and to show how the work of the various departments are all integral to Librarian Engagement Framework..

The Liaison Advisory Committee, charged to review new and existing librarian engagement assignments, will take librarian expertise and preferences into consideration in making such assignments. It should be noted though, that decisions about the requirements of the librarian's role are made first and foremost because of organizational needs. Personal preferences, therefore, cannot always be satisfied.

Framework Values

Librarianship is collaborative by nature. The Libraries are an important hub, serving as the intellectual nexus of the campus, engaging with our communities, and connecting them to a wealth of resources and services, and to one another. Collections and services evolve through collaborations and relationships. Above all, this Framework is dedicated to outreach, advocacy, and engagement, supporting the campus goal of making UMass Amherst a destination and investment of choice. The values that inform this Program include:

- **Commitment to people**, to a diversity of ideas, groups, and individuals, and to the communities that comprise the University of Massachusetts and the Commonwealth
- **Commitment to knowledge**, intellectual freedom, life-long learning, and the principles of higher education
- **Commitment to our profession**, placing a value on our integrity, high level of service, and our professional values and ethics
- **Commitment to one another**, expressed through an inclusive and collaborative work environment that prizes flexibility, innovation, creativity, personal initiative, and persistence.
- **Commitment to embracing change** by seeking out, learning about, and trying out new ideas and technologies, in order to enrich and improve the education experience of our community and ourselves.

Framework Outline

Outreach, advocacy, and engagement are the guiding principles and overarching foci of the Framework and are expected of *all librarians*. Responsibilities and core activities include:

- Initiating and facilitating ongoing dialog with faculty and students about resource needs and service expectations.
- Communicating regularly with faculty, students, and staff to develop and maintain strong and productive working relationships.
- Speaking knowledgeably about and promoting library services and issues.
- Keeping current on curricular initiatives and proposed programmatic changes.
- Working closely with faculty and students to understand their changing workflows and patterns of scholarly communication.
- Using data to inform support for faculty and students

Best practice examples:
- o Meeting regularly (at least once per semester) with faculty in assigned areas.
- o Participating in department meetings, activities, and events such as seminars, colloquia, and conferences.
- o Seeking professional development opportunities in areas of specialization (e.g., participating in scholarly societies and associations).

W:\committes&wrkgrps\LiaisonCouncil\liaison responsibilities\librarian_engagement+program+v.3_042215   4

     o Partnering with researchers on projects and/or grants.

     o Participating in departmental, college, institute and campus committees.

     o Sharing information concerning colleges, departments, programs, institutes/centers, faculty senate, and other relevant organizations (i.e., Five Colleges, Boston Library Consortium, etc.) with library colleagues.

     o Engaging in scholarly pursuits through research and coursework

     o Reviewing and using library data relevant to assigned areas.

Additional *priorities* are outlined below. As always, librarians and their supervisor will develop priorities based on departmental and individual goals and the strategic goals of the Libraries. The priorities articulate a wide range of potential activities depending on the librarian's assignment(s).

1. ***Teaching and learning:*** Design and deliver pedagogically appropriate instruction for library users that supports University curricula and learning outcomes. Responsibilities and core activities include:

- Engaging with faculty and teaching assistants/associates in programmatically integrating metaliteracy[1] concepts into the curriculum.
- Delivering and assessing effective instructional sessions[2]. Use sound instructional design practice to develop learning materials and instructional programs.
- Engaging in reflective teaching through the use of instructional improvement tools such as peer evaluation or teaching portfolios. Participate in Center for Teaching and Faculty Development (CTFD), IT Academic Computing, and other professional development programs to improve instructional and assessment techniques.
- Analyzing current teaching and research trends and materials in assigned department(s).

Best practice examples:

     o Examining the schedule of classes each semester to identify foundational, research methods, and capstone courses; contacting appropriate faculty to discuss how the Libraries can improve programmatic support.

     o Instructing or co-instructing research methods courses.

     o Meeting with departmental undergraduate and graduate program directors on a regular basis to keep current on instructional changes and needs.

     o Keeping current with new pedagogical techniques.

---

[1] According to Thomas P. Mackey and Trudi Jacobson, "Metaliteracy is an overarching and self-referential framework that integrates emerging technologies and unifies multiple literacy types," for example, information literacy, visual literacy, media literacy, etc. For more in-depth coverage of this subject, see: "Reframing Information Literacy as a Metaliteracy," an article by Thomas P. Mackey and Trudi E. Jacobson, which was published in the January 2011 issue of *College & Research Libraries*.

[2] Instructional sessions includes classroom sessions and individual research consultations.

- o Creating student learning outcomes for library instruction sessions, using assessment methods to evaluate student learning, and using results to improve instruction.
- o Collaborating with other campus partners to ensure that online course and subject guides are integrated into learning management systems.

2. *Research and client services:* Provide in-depth, specialized consultations and workshops for users. Responsibilities and core activities include:

- Offering expert assistance to users.
- Developing user capabilities with finding, evaluating, and using information and pertinent technologies.
- Providing assistance and consultations in using specialized databases, citation management, data services, copyright, metadata schema, digital preservation, finding aids, and other library research tools.
- Assisting with accreditation preparation and benchmarking activities
- Documenting and analyzing data on service transactions.
- Contributing to the identification of user needs and the measurement of outcomes of reference, teaching, learning, and research services.
- Assisting with the preparation of grant applications and systematically reviewing the literature
- Providing assistance and consultations in multimedia production and support of technologies available through the libraries.

Best practice examples:

- o Participating in staffing email, chat, and other virtual services or service desks as appropriate
- o Holding office hours in a department, centers, and institutes.
- o Supporting use of citation management products (e.g., *RefWorks*).
- o Partnering with data producers and repository contributors to help manage, disseminate, and curate research data.
- o Holding workshops to teach members of the UMass community how to use various library technologies and tools.

3. *Content management and scholarly communication :* Develop, manage, and curate collections to support teaching, learning and research. Responsibilities and core activities include:

- Selecting, acquiring, and managing content in assigned subject and functional areas.
- Strategically assessing and making data informed decisions regarding the acquisition, retention, and preservation of content
- Collaborating with appropriate library staff on arrangement, description, cataloging, and provision of access to content.
- Assisting in content recruitment and identifying digital resources that require long-term preservation and merit sustained access.

W:\committes&wrkgrps\LiaisonCouncil\liaison responsibilities\librarian_engagement+program+v.3_042215   6

Best practice examples:

o Selecting, describing and making accessible material in all formats (print, manuscripts, digital, data sets, fixed and streaming multimedia), to serve the current and future research, teaching, and learning needs of UMass Amherst clientele.
o Analyzing ILL borrowing to inform changes to approval plans, demand driven acquisitions profiles and collection practices, and note trends in user resource needs.
o Educatingfaculty and graduate students about their rights as authors (e.g., that they can alter contracts to include retaining rights to distribute their own work in classes and on personal websites).
o Advocating with authors and editors for sustainable models of scholarly communication.
o Keeping current with research in disciplines and areas of study and communicating emerging trends in modes of scholarship with library colleagues.
o Making faculty and graduate students aware of alternative publication models in their discipline.
o Serving as a liaison between the IR and campus constituents in colleges, departments and institutes to foster adoption of the IR as a scholarly communication tool.
o Working actively to recruit and make discoverable the scholarly output of the UMass Amherst and/or local community
o Working actively to recruit and make discoverable unique and rare resources, regardless of format.
o Understanding basic copyright principles and recognizing basic areas of application (e.g., fair use scenarios and face-to-face teaching exemptions).
o Educating faculty, graduate students, and campus administrators about scholarly communication issues.
o Working closely with faculty and students to understand their changing workflows and scholarly communications patterns; assist in the development and creation of tools and services to facilitate scholarly communication.

Endorsed by the Senior Management Group, May 7, 2015

W:\committes&wrkgrps\LiaisonCouncil\liaison responsibilities\librarian_engagement+program+v.3_042215   7

SELECTED RESOURCES

Books, Chapters, and Journal Articles

Andrade, Ricardo, and Raik Zaghloul. "Restructuring Liaison Librarian Teams at the University of Arizona Libraries, 2007–2009." *New Library World* 11, no. 7–8 (2010): 273–86. http://www.emeraldinsight.com/doi/abs/10.1108/03074801011059911?journalCode=nlw

Anthony, Kristin. "Reconnecting the Disconnects: Library Outreach to Faculty as Addressed in the Literature." *College & Undergraduate Libraries* 17, no. 1 (2010): 79–92. http://www.tandfonline.com/doi/abs/10.1080/10691310903584817

Bennett, Miranda Henry. "The Benefits of Non-Library Professional Organization Membership for Liaison Librarians." *The Journal of Academic Librarianship* 31, no. 1 (2011): 46–53. http://www.sciencedirect.com/science/article/pii/S0099133310002570

Carpan, Carolyn. "The Importance of Library Liaison Programs." *College & Undergraduate Libraries* 18, no. 1 (2011): 104–10. http://www.tandfonline.com/doi/abs/10.1080/10691316.2011.550536?src=recsys

Crawford, Alice. *New Directions for Academic Liaison Librarians.* Oxford, UK: Chandos Publishing, 2012.

Crossno, Jon E., Claudia H. DeShay, Mary Ann Huslig, Helen G. Mayo, and Emily F. Patridge. "A Case Study: The Evolution of 'Facilitator Model' Liaison Program in an Academic Medical Library." *Journal of the Medical Library Association* 100, no. 3 (2012): 171–75. http://www.researchgate.net/publication/230645855_A_case_study_the_evolution_of_a_facilitator_model_liaison_program_in_an_academic_medical_library

Dahl, Candice. "Library Liaison with Non-Academic Units: A New Application for a Traditional Model." *Partnership: The Canadian Journal of Library and Information Practice and Research* 2, no. 1 (2007): 1–12. http://ecommons.usask.ca/handle/10388/27

Hahn, Karla. "Introduction: Positioning Liaison Librarians for the 21st Century." *Research Library Issues: A Bimonthly Report from ARL, CNI, and SPARC*, no. 265 (August 2009): 1–2. http://publications.arl.org/rli265/

Henry, Jo. "Academic Library Liaison Programs: Four Case Studies." *Library Review* 61, no. 7 (2012): 485–96. http://www.emeraldinsight.com/doi/abs/10.1108/00242531211288236

Kenney, Anne R. "From Engaging Liaison Librarians to Engaging Communities." *College & Research Libraries* 76, no. 3 (2015): 386–91. crl.acrl.org/content/76/3/386.full.pdf

Kesselman, Martin A., and Sarah Barbara Watstein. "Creating Opportunities: Embedded Librarians." *Journal of Library Administration* 49, no. 4 (2009): 383–400. http://www.tandfonline.com/doi/abs/10.1080/01930820902832538

Kozel-Gains, Melissa A., and Richard A. Stoddart. "Experiments and Experiences in Liaison Activities: Lessons from New Librarians in Integrating Technology, Face-to-Face, and Follow Up." *Collection Management* 34, no. 2 (2009): 130–42. http://www.tandfonline.com/doi/abs/10.1080/01462670902729150

Mack, Daniel C., and Gary W. White (Eds). *Assessing Liaison Librarians: Documenting Impact for Positive Change.* PIL #67, Chicago: Association of College & Research Libraries, 2014.

Malenfant, Kara J. "Leading Change in the System of Scholarly Communication: A Case Study of Engaging Liaison Librarians for Outreach to Faculty." *College & Research Libraries* 71, no. 1 (2010): 63–76. crl.acrl.org/content/71/1/63.full.pdf

Moniz, Richard, Jo Henry, and Joe Eshleman. *Fundamentals for the Academic Liaison.* Chicago: ALA Editions, 2014.

Moniz, Richard, and Jean Moats (Eds.). *The Personal Librarian: Enhancing the Student Experience.* Chicago: ALA Editions, 2014.

Pasek, Judith E. "Organizing the Liaison Role: A Concept Map." *C&RL News* 76, no. 4 (2015): 202–05. http://crln.acrl.org/content/76/4/202.short?rss=1&ssource=mfr

Rodwell, John, and Linden Fairbairn. "Dangerous Liaisons? Defining the Faculty Liaison Librarian Service Model, its Effectiveness and Sustainability." *Library Management* 29, no. 1–2 (2008): 116–24. http://www.emeraldinsight.com/doi/abs/10.1108/01435120810844694

Shumaker, David. "Who Let the Librarians Out? Embedded Librarianship and the Library Manager." *Reference & User Services Quarterly* 48, no. 3 (Spring 2009): 239–42, 257. https://www.questia.com/library/journal/1G1-197105958/who-let-the-librarians-out-embedded-librarianship

Sievers-Hill, Arlene Moore. "Building Library Collections in the 21st Century: The Finer Points of Being an Acquisition Librarian/Library Liaison." *Against the Grain* 22, no. 5 (2010): 80–82. http://docs.lib.purdue.edu/atg/vol22/iss5/36/

Silver, Isabel D. "Outreach Activities for Liaison Librarians." *Reference and User Services Quarterly* 45, no. 2 (2014): 8–14. https://www.questia.com/library/journal/1G1-408647766/outreach-activities-for-librarian-liaisons

Thull, James, and Mary Anne Hansen. "Academic Library Liaison Programs in US Libraries: Methods and Benefits." *New Library World* 110, no. 11–12 (2009): 529–40. http://www.emeraldinsight.com/doi/abs/10.1108/03074800911007541

Reports

Auckland, Mary. *Reskilling for Research: An Investigation into the Role and Skills of Subject Liaison Librarians Required to Effectively Support the Evolving Information Needs of Researchers.* London: Research Libraries UK, January 2012. http://hdl.voced.edu.au/10707/204093

Jaguszewski, Janice, and Karen Williams. *New Roles for New Times: Transforming Liaison Roles in Research Libraries.* Washington, DC: Association of Research Libraries, August 2013. http://www.arl.org/component/content/article/6/2893

Kenney, Anne R. *Leveraging the Liaison Model: From Defining 21st Century Research Libraries to Implementing 21st Century Research Universities.* Ithaka S+R, New York: Ithaka S+R, March 2014. http://www.sr.ithaka.org/blog/leveraging-the-liaison-model-from-defining-21st-century-research-libraries-to-implementing-21st-century-research-universities/

Latta, Gail F. *Liaison Services in ARL Libraries.* SPEC Kit 189, Washington, DC: Association of Research Libraries, November/December 1992. http://babel.hathitrust.org/cgi/pt?id=mdp.39015029544189;view=1up;seq=5

Logue, Susan, John Ballestro, Andrea Imre, and Julie Arendt. *Liaison Services.* SPEC Kit 301, Washington, DC: Association of Research Libraries, October 2007. http://publications.arl.org/Liaison-Services-SPEC-Kit-301/

Made in the USA
Charleston, SC
06 November 2015